Miniature Quilts
Connecting New & Old Worlds

By Tina M. Gravatt

American Quilter's Society

P. O. Box 3290 • Paducah, KY 42002-3290

DEDICATION

This book is dedicated to

Anonymous

who made functional, beautiful, elegant, and fun quilts.

Gravatt, Tina M.
   Miniature quilts : connecting the new and old worlds / by Tina M.
Gravatt
      p.   cm.
   Includes bibliographical references.
   ISBN 0-89145-877-8
   1. Quilting--Patterns. 2. Patchwork--Patterns. 3. Miniature
quilts. 4. Quilting--Europe--History. I. Title.
TT835.G7315 1996
746.46'041--dc20   96-28026
                                                      CIP

Additional copies of this book may be ordered from:

American Quilter's Society
P. O. Box 3290
Paducah, KY 42002-3290

@$14.95. Add $2.00 for postage & handling.

Copyright: Tina M. Gravatt, 1996

This book or any part thereof may not be reproduced
without the written consent of the Publisher.

Printed in the U.S.A. by Image Graphics

PREFACE

In 1981 I was invited to teach and lecture in Scotland. Being a student of American history, I chose to give a slide and lecture presentation about the uniqueness of the American repetitive quilt block format. It was well received and in 1983 I taught and lectured in England. Since then I have been fortunate to have the opportunity to return to Britain most every year. Last year I added Wales and Northern Ireland to my list of countries.

Visiting Britain and sharing quilting with women, and a few men, is very exciting and fulfilling. As I have taught them what I know, they have done the same for me. I'd like to thank them all for sharing their knowledge.

This past year I visited Beamish, the North of England Open Air Museum in County Durham, England. On a four-hundred-acre-site, life in England just prior to World War I has been re-created through the removal of actual dwellings from their original sites in the north of England to Beamish. There is a working colliery (coal mine), colliery village with pit cottages where the miners lived and the women made quilts, train station, steam fair (carousel, rides, etc.), farms, and a town's main street complete with garage, sweet shop, pub, and town houses, several of which have bedrooms that display period quilts.

It was here that I met Rosemary Allan, the senior keeper, who allowed me to view the documentation and photographs of their entire quilt collection. Afterward, she personally escorted me into an "on site" bedroom where some twenty of the quilts were draped over one bed. It was a thrilling experience to be able to actually touch quilts (through cotton gloves) which I had only previously seen in photographs from the museum's excellent catalog (written by Ms. Allan). Her warmth and knowledge made my research trip extra special.

While teaching at the "Gulf States Quilter's Convention" in the spring of 1993, I met Vania Cole, a South African who lived in Wales. We struck up a brief friendship and she invited me to come and visit her if I had spare time while on my next trip in Britain. Since her home was small, she asked her friend, Clare Claridge, to be my hostess. Little did I know when I stepped off the train to meet her that Clare and I would become fast friends. She is a quilting teacher who travels all over the hills and valleys of southern Wales bringing "the word" – *quilting* – to women of all ages and socioeconomic conditions. Her enthusiasm has spurred quilting groups, and quilt shows, and given a great deal of emotional support to women, some of whom live rather isolated lives.

Clare introduced me to Christine Stevenson, curator of the textile collection at the Welsh Folk Museum. Like the Beamish, it is primarily an outdoor facility, but it illustrates life from the time of the Celts to the present. My favorite building was Rhyd-y-car, a group of six houses furnished as they would have been in 1805, 1855, 1895, 1925, 1955, and 1985. It was fascinating to see the development of furniture styles and interior decoration, as well as the way the physical space was readapted during each time period. There are many quilts at the Welsh Folk Museum and every building with a bed has at least one quilt on display.

Clare arranged for us to visit two of the storage rooms for the "on site" quilts, and I was allowed to photograph at will. Her strong arms were invaluable during these sessions, and especially her knowledge of the quilting and textile history of Wales.

The information in this book was not restricted to museum visitations only. I have read everything I could find on Europe's quilting history. But, unfortunately, I can only read the English language, and with some sources I had to use a dictionary to translate the captions which accompanied photos. My friend Sheila Rosenfield and I used a Swedish dictionary and her scientific German skills (gained in college more than a few years ago) to struggle through the photo captions in Åsa Wettre's book, *Gamla Svenska Lapptäcken*, which was invaluable to me in my research on Swedish quilts.

Another author of importance is An Moonen, who was the textile curator at the Openluchtmuseum in Arnhem, the Netherlands. Her book, *Quilts, Enn Nederlandse Traditie*, is written in both Dutch and English and is an invaluable source on that country's quilting history.

Ms. Moonen gave Helen Kelley and I a behind-the-scenes tour of the museum's quilt collection.

We were driven to a World War II German radar bunker on the outskirts of town. Inside the double building (first you go up, then you go down, then you go up again) was a quilt and textile collection that covered the seventeenth, eighteenth, nineteenth, and twentieth centuries. Quilted silk petticoats, pieced hexagon, triangle, and Log Cabin quilts, Indian printed Palampores, and other items too numerous to mention were unfolded for us to enjoy. She even found a miniature doll cradle and quilt from 1850 to show me. Ms. Moonen was most generous with both her time and knowledge. Unfortunately, ill health has prevented her from continuing in her position at the museum.

I met a free-lance reporter for *Handwerken Zonder Gretzen* magazine while on my first teaching trip to the Netherlands, who has since become a very dear friend. Sietske de Ruiter van der Leij specializes in writing articles about embroideries, costumes, and various textiles. She interviewed me about my work and we have kept in touch ever since. We are both fond of flea markets and antique malls where nothing escapes our investigation. Whenever possible, she sends me lovely treats of old trims, embroideries, and silk fabrics. She is also responsible for introducing me to An Moonen.

A very special and important friend is Carolyn Plumb. We met on one of the most difficult days of my life when I was forced to leave home with one suitcase and two children. Carolyn had come to America to visit quilt shops and meet quilting groups. I took her to an area quilt show, shared lunch with her and my quilting group, and listened while she told us all about England and its quilting traditions. She has become like a sister to me. Carolyn is always ready by phone or letter to answer questions and to assist in my research in any way she can. She is an experienced teacher, quilter, textile researcher, and a founding member of the Quilter's Guild in Great Britain. Carolyn loves to go to antique shows and shops looking for treasures. This past year she found a collapsible cast iron and gilded wood bed for my collection. It will enable me to show off my miniature Victorian quilts to their best advantage.

My second most special friend (only because we haven't known each other as long) is Liesbeth Spaans-Prins, who arranged for and organized my first classes in the Netherlands. She has since moved to France where she operates a luxurious bed and breakfast near Cognac. Just this year, I had the unexpected opportunity to visit with Liesbeth and her husband, Albert. I stayed at their B & B and they drove me over a thousand miles to Provence and to Paris to research French quilting history and textiles. They translated the tour guide's words, signage, and sorted through menus and tourist information to find places of special interest for me. They introduced me to French quilters and Liesbeth translated my entire slide and lecture program for her students. There aren't words to describe their generosity.

Without sounding too much like a nepotist, I need to thank two very dear people who live in Britain – my daughter, Lisa Adele McBryde, and her hubby, Craig. Lisa had the foresight, although it wasn't on her mind at the time, to move to Scotland in order to provide me a bed and home cooking! Craig is a kind, humorous, and supportive fellow who has the good sense to encourage his mother-in-law's quilting habit. Whenever I visit, Craig always asks to see my newest work, and he even takes my quilting books to work to show his "mates."

When Lisa was little she used to think up the most perfect titles for my quilts, travel with me to fabric shops, and offer suggestions as to which fabrics looked best together. Now, as an adult, she assists with arranging my British schedule. It is a monumental task to coordinate six to eight guilds into a five or six week period. There are numerous phone calls and letters about classes, programs, travel. It is a great relief to me to have someone who is reliable and efficient to organize my schedule.

Finally, I would like to acknowledge the help of all those quilters and nonquilters whom I've met who have donated old fabric, lace, trims, old towels, etc. to my stash of vintage fabrics. Without their help, quilts like the English Diamond Hexagons could not have been made. I am fortunate that "the good old days" when people helped people still exist. Patsy Buck donated two entire strips of late nineteenth century patchwork blocks from a quilt top that had been in her family. Linda McNeil, a quilter and an artist, donated a piece of 1840's fabric. Their generosity and that of many others enables me to be as successful as I am in re-creating the history of quilting in miniature.

THANKS to everyone!

CONTENTS

INTRODUCTION..6

GENERAL INFORMATION 7

PART I – THE QUILTS & THEIR HISTORIES 10

CONNECTING THE NEW & OLD WORLDS COLOR PLATE SECTION 17

PART II – CHAPTER 1 – WHOLE-CLOTH QUILTS 22

    DUTCH WHOLE-CLOTH QUILT WITH BORDERS 22

    WELSH WHOLE-CLOTH QUILT 24

    PAISLEY SHAWL QUILT 25

    TOILE DE JOUY QUILT 26

    PROVENÇAL WEDDING QUILT 27

CHAPTER 2 – MEDALLIONS OR FRAMED QUILTS....................30

    DURHAM APPLIQUÉ MEDALLION QUILT 30

    WELSH SCRAP MEDALLION QUILT 38

    SWEDISH FRAMED MEDALLION 39

CHAPTER 3 – STRIPPY QUILTS....................................41

    PROVENÇAL STRIPPY QUILT 41

    SWEDISH STRIPPY QUILT 42

CHAPTER 4 – HEXAGONS..43

    HEXAGON DIAMONDS 43

    TRIP AROUND THE WORLD HEXAGONS QUILT..................45

CHAPTER 5 – LOG CABIN..47

    SCOTTISH RED & WHITE LOG CABIN QUILT..................47

    SWEDISH LOG CABIN VARIATION QUILT 49

CHAPTER 6 – PROVENÇAL ONE PATCH QUILT....................51

CHAPTER 7 – TUMBLING BLOCKS OR BABY'S BLOCKS 52

CHAPTER 8 – ELIZABETH SANDERSON STAR QUILT 55

CHAPTER 9 – OCTAGONS..59

BIBLIOGRAPHY..61

MUSEUMS..63

INTRODUCTION

"There is nothing new except what is forgotten."
Madamoiselle Bertin, 1744–1813
(Milliner to Marie Antoinette)

While we may often quote the Bible, "There is nothing new under the sun," we don't think about what these words really mean. Most everything we do owes a debt to that which came before. Architecture is a prime example. Each skyscraper that is built is based on a foundation not of stone or steel but on the tower houses of Scotland, the fairytale castles of France and Germany, and the magnificent cathedrals of the Renaissance. The father of the modern skyscraper was Louis Sullivan, the great architect of turn-of-the-century Chicago and teacher of Frank Lloyd Wright. Nothing we create is independent of that which came before.

The same is true about quilts and quilting. America did not invent patchwork, appliqué, or the quilting stitch. These techniques had been in use for centuries before there was a United States. Averil Colby wrote in her book, *Quilting*, about the use of quilted undergarments beneath the medieval coats of chain mail. Appliquéd images on a Scytho-Siberian rug date to between the first century B.C. and second century A.D. There is a carved statue of an Egyptian pharaoh from circa 3400 B.C. that appears to wear a quilted outer garment.

This book endeavors to show the connections between the quilts of Europe and our own quilting history. There isn't a lot of written reference material available, except for Elizabeth Hake (1937), Mavis FitzRandolph (1954), Averil Colby (1958, 1972), and more recently, Dorothy Osler, Janet Rae, and Schnuppe von Gwinner. Now, historians are emerging in Sweden, the Netherlands, Wales, England, and various other countries to study their needlework arts and to share their findings with those of us on this side of the Atlantic.

Most of the material for this book came from my study of antique quilts in various European countries. We must remember, however, that the number of surviving quilts, in Europe or America, is incredibly small compared to the number of quilts that were actually made. Their purpose was to provide warmth and comfort. They had to be laundered and used daily in certain countries. It is inevitable that most quilts did not survive to educate us as to the styles and fashions of the day. It is from these few surviving examples that we draw our historical information.

European quilts share many styles and patterns with American quilts, while other features are unique to each country and region. Incidentally, one of the hardest concepts for those of us in the United States to understand is that a country as small as the Netherlands can have many regional differences. Colors and fabrics change from area to area, and styles are severely restricted by local customs and traditions. Britain is made up of four separate and distinct countries and should never be considered as only one.

You will notice that I start this book with five whole-cloth quilts representing France, the Netherlands, and Wales. Based on the high percentage of surviving whole-cloth quilts, I could have made one for each and every country. Why are there so many quilts in this simple style? The yardage needed to make a quilt is a significant monetary outlay. Often, whole-cloth quilts are made from exotic or expensive goods, which might indicate a reason to handle them more carefully. Perhaps they were only used on special occasions. Whatever the reason(s), we are thankful to past generations for preserving these treasures for us.

I have included medallion quilts because of the large number of surviving quilts made in this format. They are easy quilts to make. The quiltmaker puts something in the center and keeps adding borders until the desired size is reached. Of course, the pattern chosen for the center and the borders can lead to some of the most intricate and stunning examples of needlework to be found in early English quilts. In Averil Colby's book, *Patchwork Quilts*, there is one medallion quilt that dates to 1760 – 1785 which looks like marquetry work. It is said that the quilt was by a young man from the Isle of Jersey who designed a set of bedroom chairs and the quilt to go with it. However, he left the needlework to his fiancé, a Miss Shepherd, who made the quilt.

The only appliquéd quilt in this book is a medallion quilt whose origin is mid-nineteenth century English. It is a stunning work of art. I would have included more appliqué quilts, but among surviving antique quilts, appliqué quilts like this one do not seem to be as prevalent in Europe as in America. There are many *broderie perse* quilts that are made from cut-out fabric motifs which were appliquéd onto plain or pattern backgrounds. But including quilts of this style in a pattern book would require that we all had a common source for in-scale and proportion-applicable motifs. We don't!

I have also included several American favorites, although the examples in this book have a decided non-American flare.

I hope you will be inspired to make some of these quilts and to add some miniature European treasures to your collection of little quilts.

GENERAL INFORMATION

VINTAGE AND OLD FABRICS

Old fabrics can be found for sale from many of the vendors at the larger quilt conventions and at some of the booths in large antique malls. The older the fabric, the more expensive it will be. When buying old fabric, consider the possibility that after it is cleaned it may not have enough tensile strength to withstand the handling necessary to be used in making a quilt.

If possible, when the old fabric is purchased, ask if it has been washed or cleaned. Even if it has, I recommend that you clean it again. This way you will know the quality of the job. If the fabric can be washed, use ORVUS® soap. It is a pure soap that is used by museums for cleaning textiles and painted wood. Wash the fabric by hand, using the hottest water your hands can tolerate. The water must be hot, because if the fabric is not colorfast, you will need to know now, and not later when the completed quilt needs laundering. Do not abrade the fabric by rubbing or wringing it out. Be gentle. Wet fabric is much more fragile than dry fabric. Rinse the fabric thoroughly; any residual soap or dirt in an old fabric will shorten its life.

After laundering, dry the fabric by laying it out flat on a towel to dry. Do not use an automatic dryer as it will expose the fabric to excessive heat. When the fabric is dry, test it to be sure that the fibers are strong enough to use safely. I do this by *gently* tugging at the fabric both on the straight and cross grain. If you feel it pull or begin to give, discard it. It shouldn't be used to make a quilt as it will not withstand the stress that quilting produces. Sometimes an old fabric can seem stable, but when you begin to quilt it will start to tear. If this happens, either discard the project, tear out and replace the poor quality fabric, or appliqué a patch over the damaged area.

If old or vintage fabric can't be hand washed, you can attempt to have it dry cleaned, if you are willing to risk the damage that harsh chemicals may cause.

Do not use old and vintage fabrics indiscriminately. Use appropriate colors and patterns for the time period you are trying to emulate. Vintage 1930's fabrics belong in a quilt that was popular at that time period. Caution should be used when working with fabrics prior to the 1890's. The older the fabric, the more probable it is that the tensile strength or colorfastness may not be equal to your recycling task.

Old silks can be obtained by shopping in thrift shops and antique malls. Men's ties are ideal for miniature quilt projects. Ties are constructed using the bias of the fabric, which may present some problems when you go to use it. To compensate, I prefer to use tie silk for projects that are constructed by the English paper-piecing method. Basting tie silk to paper stabilizes the silk and makes the pieces easier to handle.

Have the ties professionally laundered or try it yourself, using Orvus® soap in cool water. As with cotton fabrics, if any of the dye runs, discard the fabric. Dry flat, press carefully so as not to stretch the fabric. Do not use any areas that have remained soiled or stained.

REPRODUCTION VINTAGE FABRICS

Since not everyone has access to antique malls, thrift shops, and large quilting conventions, the current fad for reproduction vintage fabrics can supply an old-fashioned look without the costs and hazards. There are 1930's style fabrics, late nineteenth century prints, and the fabulous collection of reprints from the quilts in the Smithsonian Institution's collection. While these fabrics are American, they are indicative of the colors and styles that were popular in all the quilting countries of Europe.

PAPER PIECING

This technique is used when precision is paramount. It takes a little extra time but guarantees a high-quality result in the completed quilt. Traditionally, paper piecing has been used when constructing hexagons or other unusually shaped pieces, but it can be used for any shape.

First, cut papers to the exact size of the completed patch. In the last two centuries when paper piecing was the only correct way to construct patchwork, paper was made from cotton rags. The result was a quality item with body and stiffness that was just perfect for stabilizing the fabric patches. However, "rag" paper as it is known today is very expensive and not readily available. The paper we have in everyday use is too thin for handling the small pieces necessary in a miniature quilt. I prefer to use file or index cards. They are a little stiffer and hold their edge for better accuracy. I especially like the file cards that can be bought in discount chain stores. They are a bit thinner than the ones from the stationery stores, and are therefore easier to stitch through.

After cutting out the papers, cut your fabric pieces, adding the standard ¼" seam allowance to all edges. I prefer to make a plastic template for the papers and a separate template for the fabric pieces.

Place the paper in the middle of the wrong side of the fabric patch and fold the fabric edges over the paper, Fig. 1. The edges are then basted in place, using quilting thread for basting. I find that quilting thread is thicker and therefore easier to remove. After all the pieces are basted, assembly begins.

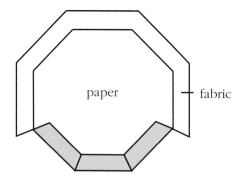

Figure 1. The fabric edges are folded over the paper.

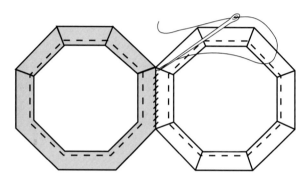

Figure 2. A whipstitch is used to join pieces together.

With right sides together, whipstitch seams together using all-purpose sewing thread in a matching color, Fig. 2. Try not to stitch through the papers. About ten stitches to a half-inch are adequate. After all seams are assembled, clip threads and remove basting stitches and papers. Be careful not to clip into the fabric when removing basting stitches. Also, take care to remove all papers. If you find one when quilting the top, it will be too late to remove it!

QUILTING

In order to keep the quilting in proper perspective to the overall graphics or design of your quilt, I recommend using matching color quilting thread. When quilting straight lines, I use masking tape in a width that will allow me to quilt on either side of the tape before having to remove it. Although this technique is very useful, do not leave tape on overnight or in a location where the temperatures are high (car, attic) because the adhesive on the tape may come off onto the quilt. The tape will stretch after two or three uses. Discard and use new tape, otherwise it will distort the quilting pattern.

FINISHING

In England, Wales, Scotland, the Netherlands, France, and Sweden, the majority of the quilts do not have a separate binding. Any of the following techniques, however, may be used on your miniature.

TECHNIQUE A: The edges are folded in from the front and the back and hand sewn closed. It is best to stitch the edges together from the back of the quilt. This way the front will fold slightly towards the back making a more pleasant finish. After the edges are completed, wherever possible, stitch a row of quilting ¼" back from the edge on all sides.

TECHNIQUE B: If making a separate binding, cut bias strips ¾" wide and seam enough together to measure the total of the outside edges plus 1" to 2". Sew binding on the front of the quilt with a ¼" seam and then trim to ⅛" wide. Bring the binding over the back, tuck in the edges, and hand sew closed.

TECHNIQUE C: In the late eighteenth and early nineteenth century in America, a separate hand-loomed tape of about ½" to ¾" wide was applied to the edges of many old quilts.

This method can be emulated in miniature by the use of seam binding (preferably the older type which is quite thin and has a looser weave). Trim the quilt to even the edges and apply the seam binding over both the top and back surface of the quilt. Stitch down using a running stitch, being careful to catch all five layers. End by cutting off the binding ½" longer than needed, folding the raw edge to the inside, and slipstitching the end of the binding over the beginning edge.

TECHNIQUE D: Piping is an alternate edge treatment used in the eighteenth century, which regained popularity on certain Victorian quilts. Narrow strips of bias fabric are seamed together as if making a separate binding, but then are wrapped around a narrow cord and stitched using a basting stitch, Fig. 3. Since the cord available to you may not be the same size as mine, it is best to buy the cord and then cut the bias strips wide enough to wrap around it and still maintain a ¼" seam allowance. Anything smaller rips out too easily.

Machine stitch (it can be stitched by hand using very small stitches) the piping onto the top of the quilt, right sides together, leaving a hollow at the beginning of the cording. When you come to the end, stop stitching and cut the cord long enough to fill in the hollow from the beginning, Fig. 4. Hand sew piping edges closed. Tuck in the backing and hand sew to the piping, hiding the machine stitches.

SIGNING AND DATING

I am a firm believer in signing and dating all quilts and quilted objects. I put my name, the date, a copyright symbol (if appropriate), and the number in the series on the back of my quilts, no matter what the size. I use embroidery directly on the back of most of my quilts; a few, however, have separate labels written in indelible ink. How and what you use is up to you.

In order to further document my work, I keep a small three-ring notebook (5" x 8") with my original graphics, fabric swatches, and all pertinent information, such as beginning and completion dates, number in the series, and a photo of the quilt. This log will afford future historians a wealth of information, not only about the quilt but also about its maker, and it will provide documented proof for an insurance company in event of an accident or theft.

It only takes a few minutes to write down the facts while you are making a quilt. It is always more difficult to find time *after* a quilt has been completed.

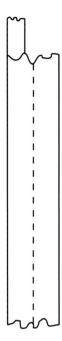

Figure 3. To make bias piping.

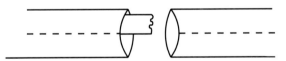

Figure 4. To assemble corded piping.

Part I

The Quilts & Their Histories

DUTCH WHOLE-CLOTH QUILT WITH BORDERS (Plate 1)

During the America's colonial period, the Dutch formed the colony of New Amsterdam in what is now the state of New York. Every schoolchild learns the story of Peter Stuyvesant, who bought the island of Manhattan from the Indians for the equivalent of $24 in beads and trinkets. However, we forget that the Dutch also settled in New Jersey and parts of Delaware where their influence is still felt.

On both sides of the Atlantic, the Dutch had a strong impact on color, pattern, and design motifs in architecture, paint, and textiles. In the sixteenth century their colonial empire was as powerful as that of Britain. They were one of several countries to form an East India trading company (others were England, France, and Sweden), which brought to Europe spices, silks, and the new rage – Indian painted and glazed cottons of many colors. (Today, the word "chintz" still denotes a very special fabric that is more costly and used more rarely than calico.)

In the seventeenth century, this new fabric became so popular that England and France both outlawed its use. Flagrant flaunting of the law by the rich and famous (Madame Pompadour among many others) helped chintz to win out and become the decorating craze of the seventeenth century. The wealthy had bedcovers or counterpanes, bed curtains, tester cloths, walls, chairs, dressing gowns, and robes made from the new "wonder" fabric!

The first whole-cloth quilt in this section is typical of the way chintz (sitz in Dutch) was used in America and the more affluent city dwellings in Holland. The fabric for this quilt is a reprint of an eighteenth century original. Note the richness of color and intricacy of design. Originally the printing was all done by hand; now French machines with high-speed rollers reprint this fabric for Den Haan and Wagenmakers in Amsterdam, the Netherlands.

Many surviving old Dutch quilts are whole cloth without borders. However, I chose to add a border to three sides of my quilt so that it would fit a four poster bed typical of the type popular in America and Europe in the mid- to late eighteenth century. I kept the fourth side borderless because it isn't visible when displayed on the bed.

It is quite common for old Dutch quilts to use a medallion arrangement for their quilting patterns. I tried to emulate this style by quilting a rectangle along the mattress dimensions, and centering an oval medallion with radiating lines between two areas of curves at the top and bottom (curves were a very popular Dutch quilting motif). The quilting is quite extensive with tulip-like flowers, vines, and rosettes.

WELSH WHOLE-CLOTH QUILT (Plate 2)

I live in Philadelphia, Pennsylvania, a city founded during America's colonial period by William Penn, who allowed religious freedom in his colony even though this freedom was denied to his fellow Quakers in Britain.

On my first visit to Glamorgan (a region in southern Wales), I stayed with Clare Claridge in a small village called Quaker's Yard. Clare explained that in the eighteenth century Quakers had sought refuge there from the persecution they had received in England. It was from this region that many Welsh Quakers came to the new world to settle in the colony of Pennsylvania. There they formed an agrarian society similar to that which they had left.

Wales has a long quilting history. So much so, it has been suggested by some historians, that it was the Welsh emigration to the area west and north of Philadelphia that influenced the quilting styles of the Amish who had also settled there. With little written evidence to explain the history of Amish quilts, we can only speculate on their origins, but there are distinct similarities in some Amish and Welsh quilt styles.

In Wales during the nineteenth century, whole-cloth and framed or medallion styles were dominant quilt designs. One of the favorite colors of Welsh quiltmakers was saffron or gold. While attending a flea market in Glasgow, Scotland, I acquired a circa 1900 – 1920 Welsh, woolen whole-cloth quilt. It was folded up on a shelf and had a replacement backing added by a skilled seamstress in the 1930's. I opened it up and the gold color still shimmered after all these years. It was hand quilted in a traditional Welsh pattern of interlocking arcs with straight lines of stitching between the rows. (The arc pattern is so popular in Wales that it can be found carved into tables, dressers, chests, and bed testers.)

I knew when I saw the quilt I would have to reproduce it in miniature. On returning home, I went through my stash of cotton fabric to find just the right shade of gold. Unfortunately, nothing seemed quite right. Then I remembered that two years before I had bought some old, yellow cotton sateen. I dug through my chest of drawers until it emerged from under the other old fabrics. Again, the shade was not exactly correct, but the sateen had a loose weave that more closely resembled the wool in the antique quilt. I decided to use the old fabric, and as I began quilting I was convinced that my choice had been the right one. The sateen was soft and supple and allowed the quilting motifs to exhibit the same qualities as those in the old quilt.

PAISLEY SHAWL QUILT (Plate 3)

While researching old Welsh quilts, I saw one that caught my imagination. It was an excellent example of using something that was no longer in fashion in a new and useful way. Two paisley shawls had been sewn together to form one side of a whole-cloth quilt.

Paisley shawls were the height of fashion in the second and third quarter of the nineteenth century. It is hard today to think of a shawl as much more than an attractive accessory. But in their heyday, these woolen garments served as giant wraps and were a substitute for an outer coat. The original designs came from the province of Kashmir in India, but were soon copied in Norwich and other cities in England. Not to be outdone by the English, the weavers in Scotland copied the paisley pattern and made the new fashion their own. Today, the city of Paisley, Scotland, has the formost collection of shawls, looms, and original weaver's patterns.

In the 1870's, more tailored clothing became fashionable, and the shawls were relegated to the old trunk in the attic, or draped over the massive Victorian and Edwardian tables in fashionably overdecorated parlors.

But in Wales, clever quilters turned some of these shawls into whole-cloth or pieced quilts. The wool was of a fine enough grade that hand quilting could be done, and the wool provided extra warmth.

I decided to reproduce this idea using two contemporarily made polyester scarves. They were about 29 inches square and printed with two distinctly different paisley patterns. I quilted around all the dominant motifs, and where the quilted areas would be more than an 1½" apart, I quilted around some of the smaller interior details. This technique of utilizing the printed motifs for the quilting pattern can also be found on some of the old chintz quilts in the Netherlands.

TOILE DE JOUY QUILT (Plate 4)

The words "toile de jouy" are generally used to describe blue and white or red and white fabric printed with pastoral scenes or neoclassical motifs. There were many French factories that produced these fabrics, but none as famous as the Oberkampf factory at Jouy-en-Josas outside Paris. Founded by two brothers, Christophe Phillippe and Frederic Oberkampf in 1761, they became known for creating the best quality fabrics of their day.

In the United States in the first quarter of the nineteenth century, everything and anything French was fashionable. Our household furnishings took on the style of Emperor Napoleon with brass decorations (ormolu) on the furniture, and beds decorated with neoclassical toile de jouy prints in which proclaimed the new interest in Pompeii and the civilizations of ancient Rome and Greece.

American wealthy and upper-middle-class quiltmakers preferred the more sophisticated two-color toile de jouy prints to the more common multicolor small calicos that were being produced by both the French and U.S. factories. Since French fabrics were expensive, they were often kept as whole panels seamed together to make a quilt.

I was able to duplicate the antique toile de jouy quilts by using one of the reproduction vintage fabrics available to today's quilters. This print is being produced by Peter Pan Fabrics Inc. in several different sizes and colors. For the quilting design, I chose to copy the simple double-line, diamond-grid quilting motif used on the nineteenth century French toile de jouy quilts on exhibit in the Museé de la Toile de Jouy in Jouy-en-Josas.

PROVENÇAL WEDDING QUILT (Plate 5)

In the south of France the sun shines on a land that inspired many of the great Impressionist painters of the nineteenth century. The colors are intense and dramatic. Azure blue water, terra-cotta tiles and pottery, fields of olive trees, citrus fruits, golden ripe wheat, and miles and miles of vineyards. It is easy to see why painters continue to be drawn to this region.

But perhaps less well known are the beautiful calico prints and bold floral scarves that make the clothing and quilts of this area distinctive. Souleiado and Les Olivades companies continue to print the eighteenth century Indian inspired cottons. The colors of these fabrics are more sharp than their American counterparts, and gives one the feeling of going back in time.

Some of these scarves were used to make wedding quilts in the mid-nineteenth century. French mothers would buy printed scarves and turn them into special quilts known as counterpointes. The scarves were white with three sides printed with a rich floral pattern. Matching fabric with the floral motif would be purchased and then sewn onto the plain side of the scarf. Sometimes an extra white border would be added. In any case, the center white area would be filled with crosshatch quilting, either in ornate double rows and cross motifs, or plain with the more usual single lines. One lovely quilt from this time period (photographed in the book *Country Quilts* by Linda Seward) has an additional border made from a quilted meandering vine.

I chose this more ornate quilt as the inspiration for my miniature but did not copy it exactly. Instead I used design motifs from three different Provençal quilts. It is impossible to exactly copy the floral fabric of almost 150 years ago, but any strong flower pattern will make a suitable border for your quilt.

DURHAM APPLIQUÉ MEDALLION QUILT (Plate 6)

Medallion quilts consist of a central design motif (pieced, appliquéd, or preprinted by cloth manufacturers for this purpose) surrounded by a series of borders or frames (as they are more commonly called in Britain). Medallions are one of the oldest styles of patchwork in Scotland, Wales, Northern Ireland, and England.

Appliqué is a more costly technique than piecing fabric remnants. The quiltmaker must purchase fabric so that all images are alike. Laying one layer on top of another is wasteful and was often saved for use only on special quilts. While more free-flowing and lighter in spirit than rigid pieced work, appliqué quilts are more carefully balanced and more sophisticated than simple patchwork designs.

One such quilt was made by Mrs. Isabella Cruddas of Rookhope in Weardale, Northumberland, England, about the year 1850. Her use of red, green, and white fabric, heavy quilting, and stylized flowers, buds, and leaves bears a strong resemblence to the appliqué quilts of the mid-nineteenth century in the mid-Atlantic and southern states of the U.S. It is easy to believe that Mrs. Cruddas may have had access to American designs and patterns. It is known that women in both the counties of Durham and Northumberland had relatives who had emigrated to the New World. Letters from two sisters who shared their quilting interests exist in the collection of Beamish, The North of England Open Air Museum.

Even though there may be a tie between Mrs. Cruddas' quilt and America, her color use, format, and borders are typical of the north of England. I endeavored to copy the quilting on the original as closely as possible; however, some modifications had to be made in the central square and behind the buds in the four center triangles. It is a difficult quilt to make, but one which should be tried by quilters who enjoy an appliqué challenge.

WELSH SCRAP MEDALLION QUILT (Plate 7)

The inspiration for my miniature quilt came from a full-size quilt that appeared in Janet Rae's book, *The Quilts of the British Isles*. It was made about 1910 in Dryswhyn, Wales. Because printed fabrics with the same patterns in different colors were used, it is quite possible that the quilt was made from draper's (salesman's) samples.

Like the paisley shawl quilts, costume affected quiltmaking. Scraps from fashionable dress prints went into a scrap bag for later use, which made the dating of scrap quilts very difficult. Sometimes scraps were kept for years and years, even from one generation to the next.

In the case of this quilt, it would appear that the maker was the wife of an owner of a dry goods store, a dressmaker, or had someone in her family who had access to sample swatches. She was very creative and used their rectangular shape to the best advantage. Her organizational skills drew the quilt together in a dramatic and pleasing effect.

SWEDISH FRAMED MEDALLION (Plate 8)

The first thing I notice when I look at an old

quilt in a book is its graphic design. How much impact does the quilt have? Do the colors contribute or detract from the first impression? Then I read the caption under the photo and ask, "Why did the quilt-maker make her/his decisions this way? Is it typical of a time period, region, or fashion of the day?"

Unfortunately, when a book is in a foreign language, I cannot as easily find an answer to my questions. Åsa Wettre's book, *Gamla Svenska Lapptäcken*, provided me with many rich ideas for miniature quilts to add to my collecion. But a Swedish dictionary does not provide the colloquial phrases and the subtleties necessary to do accurate research. Therefore, I can only tell you that the quilt[1] was made by Matilda Anderson who was born in 1860 and died in l933. She probably produced this quilt sometime around l888, the time of her wedding.

Although it is not an intricate masterpiece, it is a dramatic quilt. The colors are not fashionable today. By making use of old American fabrics from the 1870's – 1890's, I tried to be as faithful as possible to the colors in the original quilt. I supplemented the old with the newly popular plaids, imitation tickings, and hand-dyed solids. Your own color preferences would work equally well in Matilda's design.

It is important to note that quilting is not something new to Sweden. Åsa's book contains a watercolor picture from 1797 illustrating a fashionable parlor of the day with a quilting frame and two ladies busily at work. The third figure at the frame appears to be a man!

PROVENÇAL STRIPPY QUILT (PLATE 9)

Strippy quilts are easy to make and bring gay and bright colors into one's home. This style of quilt was made in all the quilting countries of Europe and in North America. Each region had its own style and distinctive qualities.

Amish bar quilts are strippys, as well as the Amish Chinese Coin pattern. In Britain, a Durham strippy immediately makes one think of quilted plaits (cables), chains, hammocks (swags), worms, bellows, and feathers.

I chose a strippy quilt from the Provençal region of France as the pattern for the next quilt. Among the traditional fabric colors in the south of France are red and yellow. They were two of the earliest colors to be printed, and could successfully be made permanent in order to last through many launderings.

Since miniature quilts are small, it is easy for them to fracture and lack design cohesiveness. In order to avoid this, I used a bright yellow fabric with a small red print and the identical design with a red background. The border is from a different red print. Although these fabrics are American nineteenth century reprints, they capture the feeling of the same time period in France.

Because strippys are easy to construct, experiment with color combinations and add one to your miniature quilt collection.

SWEDISH STRIPPY QUILT (Plate 10)

This miniature was inspired by an antique quilt in the book *Gamla Svenska Lapptäcken* by Åsa Wettre[2]. The originial quilt was reversible with light color fabric strips on one side, and dark color rectangles on the other. Åsa called it a winter and summer quilt because the coloring and mood of the quilt was as different as the seasons.

Many of the Swedish quilts illustrated in *Gamla Svenska Lapptäcken* are made with stripe or ticking-like fabrics, plaids, and checks. They possess a spontaneity that make them very cheery and pleasant.

I tried to duplicate the mood of the summer side of the quilt. I used stripes, plaids, and small print fabrics. It is a most enjoyable quilt to make because you can use whatever colors inspire you!

HEXAGON DIAMONDS (Plate 11)

"The hexagon is the most popular shape in English patchwork and the patterns made from it...are characteristic of this country's work."[3] It is for this reason that I have included two quilts using this ubiquitous shape.

Like the next pattern, Trip Around the World, the Hexagon Diamonds quilt uses the equilateral hexagon, but this is where the similarity ends. Quilts made from this shape can be arranged in a myriad of patterns and shapes. If, like me, your knowledge had been limited to Grandmother's Flower Garden quilts of the 1930's, give yourself the opportunity to expand your knowledge and try one or both of these hexagon quilts.

I find them very relaxing to make. All the hard work, cutting the papers, can be done when you are mentally sharp and in your work space. After that, wrapping the fabric, basting, and assembling the patches are "idiot" work. They are exceedingly portable and can help to entertain you through numerous baseball games, swim meets, and while you wait in doctor's offices.

I chose a circa 1835 English quilt as the inspiration for my miniature. I only had a black and white photo of one corner of the quilt that was illustrated in Averil Colby's book, *Patchwork*. The text said it was made of red, russet, brown, and yellow chintz with a muslin backgound.

I had studied enough English and American quilts from that time period to know how the quilt may have looked, and I was extemely fortunate to have enough old fabrics from the late nineteenth century with which to work. Most of them had been gifts from my students; however, the background fabric was from the 1840's and had been given to me by an artist friend. It had been passed down through several generations and measured almost ¾ yd. I had hoarded it for about four years because I dreaded cutting it up until just the right quilt came along.

As soon as I started to plan the colors and dimensions for this quilt, I knew that I had to use the 1840's fabric for the background of my small quilt.

TRIP AROUND THE WORLD HEXAGONS QUILT
(Plate 12)

The earliest known existing English patchwork quilt still on the bed for which it was designed, was made about 1708 at Levens Hall near Kendal in the Lake District. It still exists today and is a testament to patchwork's rich legacy. The patterns on this quilt are octagon, cruciform, and church windows (the English term for elongated hexagons).

Many incomplete hexagon patchwork tops exist both here and in Britain. Often we see these used in decorator books and magazines hung on walls and draped over tables. One of the most striking features of an incomplete hexagon quilt is its shape. They look like a giant pieced hexagon. I wanted to duplicate this effect with my miniature quilt but knew that the shape would be impractical for a bed. (Although I know of a full-size bed quilt found in the Virginia quilt research project that was hexagonal in shape!) Therefore, I used the Trip Around the World arrangement of concentric color rows to accent the hexagon shape. I then filled out the corners with additional partial rows of hexagons to make a more traditional quilt shape.

In my quilt, I copied nineteenth century practice and made use of 41 different fabrics! At that time cloth of all kinds was used for patchwork. As in the U.S., dress prints in floral designs, small dot prints, and chintz patterns were used. It is this use of varied fabrics that makes the old quilts so interesting. Trying to duplicate their intricacy can be difficult, but using a wide variety of prints, many of which

can be the new reprints of the old fabrics, will make the job easier.

I used mostly old fabrics for my miniature, but reprints will give you the same effect without the fear of damage to fragile materials.

SCOTTISH RED AND WHITE LOG CABIN QUILT
(Plate 13)

Fortunately for our generation, some of our ancestors had the forethought to create museums for local history which not only recorded but also preserved and exhibited life of the past in such a way that we can feel we are actually going back in time. The Ceres Folk Museum in Fife on Scotland's eastern coast is one of these museums. It is not large, but the moment you step through the low doorway, you are transported back to the late nineteenth century. The furnishings are original, and it was here that I saw my first box bed.

They were found throughout rural Scotland in both the homes of farmers and the cottages of fishermen. These beds appear to be built into the wall and completely surround their inhabitants, providing a cozy environment against a night without heat. Simply made or carved and decorated, they were the norm in most working-class homes.

It was on such a bed that I saw the inspiration for this quilt. In a small room, dimly lit by a little window, was a beautiful red and white Log Cabin quilt. It was made with the white areas forming a cross-like pattern. The border was scalloped and embroidered with white flowers and vines. The bed itself was decorated with a matching valance, and the result was a cheeriness unsurpassed by anything we could accomplish today.

Subsequently, I have learned that this stunning quilt was one of a pair! I chose to make only one of them in miniature. Like the antique, I kept the white areas dominant, but the pattern does not form as strong a cross as the originial. Instead of embroidery, I chose to add a machine-made lace edging to my border. It maintains the delicate counterbalance of the original embroidery with the bold graphics of the Log Cabin but without the work!

SWEDISH LOG CABIN VARIATION QUILT
(Plate 14)

Åsa Wettre's book, *Gamla Svenska Lapptäcken*, was invaluable to me in my research about old Swedish quilts. My miniature quilt was inspired by an "unusual" Swedish quilt made from "strings" of fabric with four Log Cabin-like blocks in the corners.[4] It was made about 1900 – 1920, and incorporates not only the Log Cabin blocks but a simplified medallion format.

The beauty in this quilt is not that of intricate patchwork patterning or fine needlework, but its simplicity and obvious practicality. Often overlooked, the simple patterns of functional quilts can be very graphic and almost resemble modern art.

Let yourself break the rule concerning grain lines; sew together a bunch of scraps and give this quilt a try.

PROVENÇAL ONE PATCH QUILT (Plate 15)

When I made this quilt I hadn't had an opportunity to travel to France, but I had been fortunate enough to find a shop in London where I could buy authentic Provençal fabrics. I know it must seem rather unusual to shop for French fabrics in England, but like many of you, I'll buy fabrics anywhere!

When I returned home, I began a study of French textiles and learned that Provence had been exempt from the eighteenth century laws restricting the printing of Indian-style prints in France. It was this exemption from the law and the access to international trade goods for cotton and dye pigments that enabled the Provençal printers and dyers of cloth to perfect the skills necessary to produce bright and vibrant fabrics.

Quilting was practiced in Provence from the eighteenth century into the twentieth. The surviving quilts are dominantly of the whole-cloth style, but I have seen a lovely quilt made entirely of pieced half-square triangles. The golds and browns in the quilt retained their original intensity and the quilt brightened the entire room where it was displayed.

My miniature quilt is made using some of the fabric I purchased that day in England. By using small squares, I created an easy way to show off my treasures. Even if you don't have authentic French fabric, you can make a stunning little quilt from American fabrics.

TUMBLING BLOCKS (Plate 16)

Although this quilt looks like it is all-American in style, the Tumbling or Baby's Block pattern was also made in Great Britain and the Netherlands during the Victorian era. British needleworkers and quiltmakers of the nineteenth century were encouraged by lady's magazines to produce fine quality decorative needlework for their richly adorned domestic interiors. Paper-pieced silk patchwork used to form intricate patterns such as cubes, blocks, and stars were perfectly suited to the wealthy Victorian life style.

From the surviving number of examples of this pattern in Britain, it would seem that this quilt was as popular there as it was on this side of the Atlantic. Its success can be attributed to several factors. Silk was easy to attain, as the mills for its production were centrally located with access to all the major rail lines, and the raw material for this commodity came from Britain's royal colony of Hong Kong.

A quilt in this pattern was made by Styne Zunderdorp, the daughter of the burgomaster (mayor) of Vlieland, for her sister's child born on December 11, 1879. It has a beautiful machine-made lace edging, variously colored silks set off by a black diamond in each cube and, surprisingly, is machine quilted. It resides in the collection of the OPENLUCHTMUSEUM in Arnhem in the Netherlands. It is a striking quilt, and although not often on display, it has a featured place on one of the many postcards that the gift shop offers for sale.

For my miniature Tumbling Blocks quilt, I used the same paper-piecing construction technique as the quiltmakers of the past. I found I could control the silk and get a more accurately pieced quilt with this method. Silk need not be hard to find. Just cut up those old men's ties with which you couldn't bear to part!

ELIZABETH SANDERSON STAR (Plate 17)

The northern English counties of Durham and Northumberland are known for their quilting traditions. Almost on the border of these two counties lies the small village of Allenheads. In the 1880's, the village shop owner, George Gardiner, became so proficient at dressing women's hats that girls would walk many miles over the fells to avail themselves of his services. He further enhanced his reputation by marking quilt tops and becoming a professional quilt "stamper."[5] He taught his wife's two nieces and a woman who was to become his most famous pupil, Elizabeth Sanderson.

Born in 1861, Elizabeth became more famous than her teacher, and unlike Gardiner, was an excellent quilter in her own right. Although she lived on a farm, she left its management to her sister while she ran her "stamping" business. She had apprentices and employees and could mark two quilt tops a day. Her style was distinctive but owed its origins to the innovations that Gardiner had begun.

Elizabeth Sanderson died in 1934, leaving a prolific and much loved legacy to quilters of the twentieth century.

Two of her favorite quilt designs were a basket pattern similar to those popular in the U.S. in the 1930's and the star quilt that follows. These were made in pink and white, medium blue and white, or turkey red and white.

I studied several old star quilts for inspiration for my quilting patterns. In the pink points of the center star are four plants that represent the British Isles. The rose is for England, the thistle for Scotland, the daffodil for Wales, and the shamrock for Ireland. I wish I could say that I was clever enough to think up this idea, but I found it on a circa 1930's quilt owned by a student of a friend of mine. On a full-size quilt, the star points are quite large and her flowers more realistic. The feathers, hammock (swags in the U.S.), and rose (rosette) in the border are typical of North Country quilts. I especially enjoyed adding the scissor pattern to the four corners. It is such an elegant and lovely interpretation of one of our most important quilting tools.

OCTAGONS (Plate 18)

We are familiar with the ubiquitous hexagon shape for patchwork in the United States. A similar shape that was popular in Britain was the octagon. With its eight sides it required even greater precision to draft, cut, and piece.

One woman who was sucessful with this pattern was Mrs. Sybil Heslop of Ovington, Northumberland, England. About the turn of the century, she pieced a full-size quilt in wools and flannels. Then, to further exhibit her skills and frugality, she pieced the backing in squares and hand quilted her work!

Winters are cold in the north of England, and this quilt would have provided excellent warmth in a room without any heat. Fortunately, it survives today in the collection of Beamish, the North of England Open Air Museum, in near perfect condition.

I was so inspired by Mrs. Heslop's artisanship and pleasing blend of colors that I chose to emulate her work. I constructed my miniature of wools and flannels but did not piece the back or hand quilt the final result. Instead I tied the quilt on the reverse.

FOOTNOTES

[1] Antique quilt in the collection of Åsa Wettre.

[2] Antique quilt in the collection of the Textil Museet in Borås.

[3] Colby, Averil. *Patchwork*. Newton Centre, MA: Charles T. Branford Co., 1958, page 40.

[4] Wettre, Åsa. *Gamla Svenska LapptÑcken*. Stockholm, Sweden: Tidens fïrlag, 1993, page 78. (Antique quilt in the collection of Åsa Wettre.)

[5] No actual stamps were involved. All designs were drawn by hand.

Connecting the New & Old Worlds

COLOR PLATE SECTION

Plate 1. *DUTCH WHOLE-CLOTH QUILT WITH BORDERS,* 23" x 29".

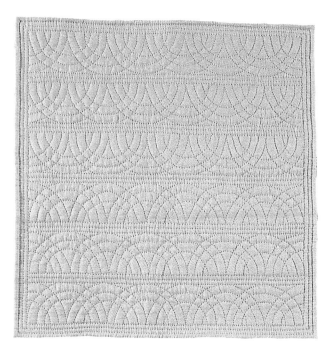

Plate 2. *WELSH WHOLE-CLOTH QUILT*, 19" x 19½".

Plate 3. *PAISLEY SHAWL QUILT*, 28¼" x 28¼".

Plate 4. *TOILE DE JOUY QUILT*, 13" x 23".

Plate 5. *PROVENÇAL WEDDING QUILT*, 16" x 24".

Plate 6. *DURHAM APPLIQUÉ MEDALLION QUILT*, 28" x 28".

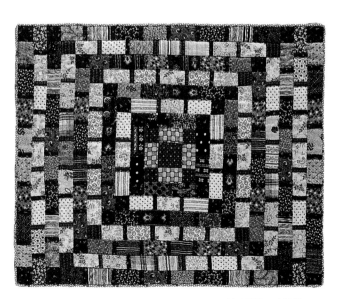

Plate 7. *WELSH SCRAP MEDALLION QUILT*, 17¾" x 21¾".

Miniature Quilts

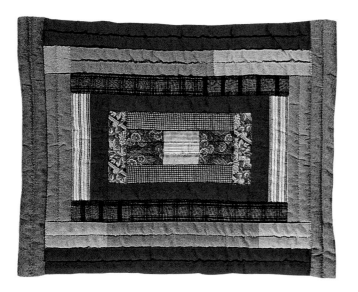

Plate 8. *SWEDISH FRAMED MEDALLION*, 14" x 18".

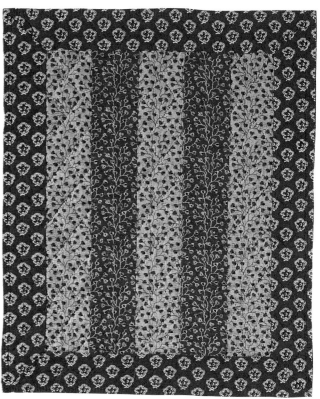

Plate 9. *PROVENÇAL STRIPPY QUILT*, 13" x 16".

Plate 10. *SWEDISH STRIPPY QUILT*, 15¾" x 19¼".

Plate 11. *HEXAGON DIAMONDS*, 24¾" x 26¼".

Plate 12. *TRIP AROUND THE WORLD HEXAGONS QUILT*, 16¾" x 20¾".

Plate 13. *SCOTTISH RED AND WHITE LOG CABIN QUILT*, 12½" x 12½".

Plate 14. *SWEDISH LOG CABIN VARIATION QUILT*, 11½" x 18".

Plate 15. *PROVENÇAL ONE PATCH QUILT*, 20¾" x 20¾".

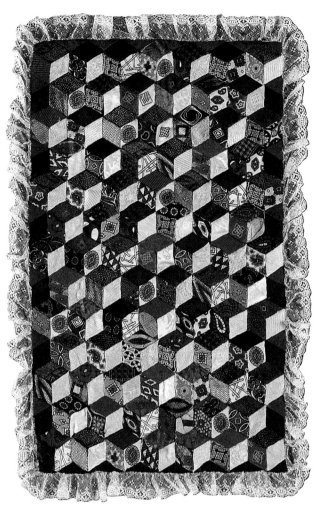

Plate 17. *ELIZABETH SANDERSON STAR*, 26" x 26".

Plate 16. *TUMBLING BLOCKS*, 8½" x 14¼".

Plate 18. *OCTAGONS*, 14½" x 14½".

Whole-Cloth Quilts

Plate 19.

YARDAGE:

1 yd. main design
¼ yd. borders
1 yd. backing

CUT:

1 – 17½" x 27" rectangle from dominant top fabric
2 strips 3½" x 23½" for side border
1 strip 3½" x 8½" wide for bottom border
1 – 24" x 30" rectangle for backing. After front is cut
   according to directions, trim backing fabric to match.
   Be sure to leave enough for seam allowances.

   *Since the quilting motifs are small and rather
   complicated, this is not a quilt for beginners.

SKILL LEVEL: *Intermediate**

**DUTCH WHOLE-CLOTH QUILT WITH BORDERS
Plate 1**

Dimensions: 23" x 29"
Number of Pieces: 4
Construction Technique: Pieced
Fabrics: Any distinctive overall pattern; borders can
   be plain or a different color but same pattern as
   the main quilt area.

DIRECTIONS:

Cut out two rectangles 4½" wide and 3½" deep
from the bottom left and right corners of the large
fabric to form cut-out corners of quilt. See diagram,
Fig. 5. Stitch borders in place.

Use a dark pen to trace the quilting patterns onto a
large sheet of tracing paper, being sure to center and
space motifs as in quilting placement diagram, Fig. 6
(page 23). Using a light box, lay the quilt top over
the quilting diagram and mark the entire surface.
Baste backing, batting, and quilt top together.

Quilting: Using neutral but matching color quilting
thread, begin quilting in the center.

Finishing: See technique "A," page 8.

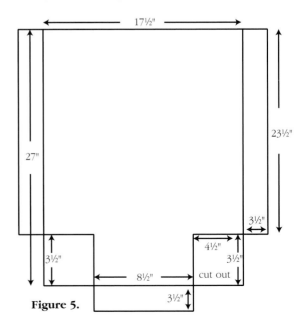

Figure 5.

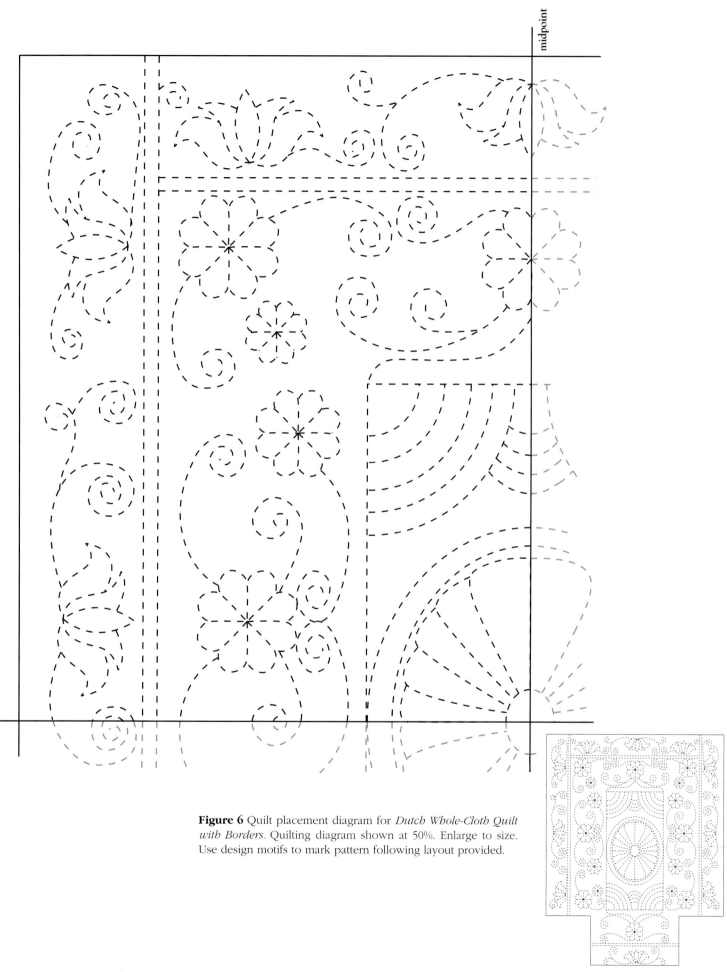

midpoint

Figure 6 Quilt placement diagram for *Dutch Whole-Cloth Quilt with Borders*. Quilting diagram shown at 50%. Enlarge to size. Use design motifs to mark pattern following layout provided.

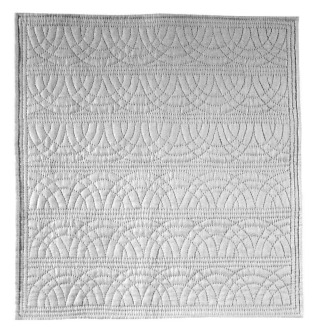

Plate 20.

YARDAGE:

1 yd.

CUT:

2 rectangles 20" x 21" (the extra fabric will allow a quilting frame to clamp in place)

WELSH WHOLE-CLOTH QUILT
Plate 2

Dimensions: 19" x 19½"
Number of Pieces: 1
Construction Technique: Not Applicable
Fabrics: Solid gold or saffron color cotton or cotton
  sateen

DIRECTIONS:

Mark the quilt top using the quilting layout diagram, Fig. 7, and arc template, Fig. 8. Masking tape can be used for the straight line quilting. There are three rows of quilting which occupy one-half inch of space between the quilted arc rows.

Finishing: See technique "A," page 8.

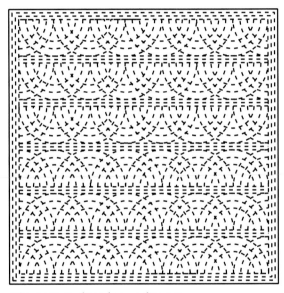

Figure 7. Quilting layout diagram.

Figure 8. Arc template.

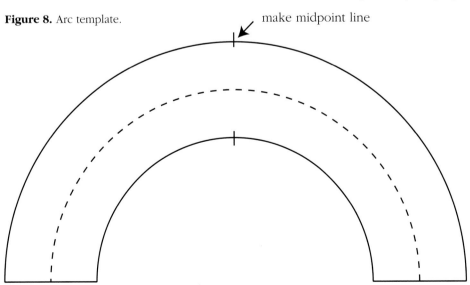

make midpoint line

Plate 21.

YARDAGE:

Scarves must be the same size

CUT:

Scarves remain intact; remove labels, but *do not* remove the narrow hems on the edges.

PAISLEY SHAWL QUILT
Plate 3

Dimensions: Will depend on the size of the purchased scarf.

Number of Pieces: 1

Construction Technique: Not Applicable

Fabrics: Two polyester scarves, either the same pattern and different colors, or two different patterns. It is best if scarf has a plain outside area that will allow it to be cut down if necessary.

DIRECTIONS:

Lay the backing scarf on the table, right side down. Lay a very thin batting on top and finish with second scarf. Since polyester is a slippery fabric, pin the three layers together with fine silk pins before basting. Take care to keep all four edges even while basting the layers together.

Quilting: Use very sharp quilting needles and check for knicks or burrs. If the needle is not smooth, it will snag the polyester threads and ruin your quilt.

Match the quilting thread to the color of each motif. Beginning in the center, quilt along the outlines of all important shapes. Be sure not to leave areas larger than 1½" square unquilted.

When the entire top has been quilted, hand stitch the edges together. Keeping the original hems will add stability to the outside of the quilt. If your quilt has shifted during the quilting process, and the outer motif design will not be ruined, cut the outside edges and square up the quilt. Tuck the raw edges in and hand stitch closed. To stabilize the edge, quilt a row of stitches ⅛" to ¼" from the edges around the circumference of the quilt.

Plate 22.

YARDAGE:

¾ yd. (these fabrics are usually directional and cannot be cut on the cross grain)

CUT:

Two rectangles 15" x 25" (the extra fabric will allow
a quilting frame to clamp in place)

TOILE DE JOUY QUILT
Plate 4

Dimensions: 13" x 23"
Number of Pieces: 1
Construction Techniques: Not Applicable
Fabrics: A red and white or blue and white print with
   allegorical figures, pastoral scenes, ruins, etc., or a flo-
   ral type print may be substituted.

DIRECTIONS:

Mark a 13" x 23" rectangle on the piece of fabric that
will become the top of the quilt. Using ¼" wide masking
tape, place a row of tape on the top from the top right
to the bottom left corner. Be sure to start and stop the
tape at the outer edge markings. Quilt along each side
of the tape. Using the same tape, place it on the quilt
top parallel and ¾" from the row last quilted. Again
quilt along both sides of the tape. Continue until the
entire quilt surface has been completed.

Repeat the above procedure beginning from the top
left to the bottom right corner. Beautiful diamonds will
be created over the entire surface. See Fig. 9.

Finishing: Since this quilt has been quilted out to the
edge, cut off excess fabric and complete the quilt using
technique "B." See page 8.

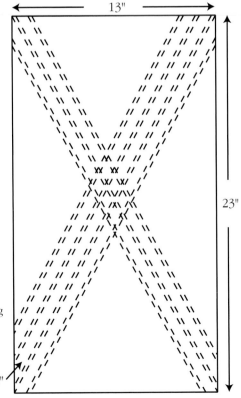

Figure 9. Diagonal quilting
lines form diamonds.

Plate 23.

YARDAGE:

¾ yd. white for center and backing

¼ yd. chintz or floral for borders (½ yd. if directional fabric)

¼ yd. for separate bias binding

CUT:

1 – 10½" x 18½" rectangle for center

2 – 3½" x 18" strips for top and bottom borders*

2 – 3½" x 26" strips for side borders*

1 – 17" x 25" rectangle for backing

*These dimensions are based on a three-inch-wide border cut on the cross grain.

PROVENÇAL WEDDING QUILT
Plate 5

Dimensions: 16" x 24" (width of outer border will determine dimensions of quilt)

Number of Pieces: 5

Constructions Techniques: Pieced

Fabrics: Cotton and chintz

DIRECTIONS:

Stitch top and bottom borders to narrow sides of the center rectangle, being sure to allow an equal extension over the two sides. In the same way, add the side borders. Miter corners and trim square.

Quilting: Draw a line 1¾" inside the seam line on all sides of the center rectangle. This space will become the inner border for the quilted vine motif. Mark the vine and leaf motif on the quilt top. Lay top and batting on backing and baste the three layers together.

Beginning at the upper left, attach ¼" wide masking tape to the surface with the top edge of the tape in the point of the upper left corner and the bottom edge of the tape in the point of the lower right corner. Quilt along both sides of tape. Place tape along the bottom quilting row and quilt one additional line, see quilting layout Fig. 10. Place tape parallel and 1" from the last quilting row and quilt along each side of the tape. Again, place tape next to the last row and quilt on the outside edge. Continue until the entire rectangle, stopping at the inner border marking, is completed.

To create the diamonds, begin diagonal rows of quilting from the upper right to the lower left, placing tape as before. When the entire rectangle has been quilted, diamonds will be formed between the double rows. Quilt from the top to the bottom point, and side to side point inside each diamond, forming a cross.

Quilt vine and leaves. The outside border is quilted on the diagonal in single rows ¾" apart beginning and parallel to each mitered corner. See quilting layout, Fig. 11.

Finishing: See technique "B," page 8.

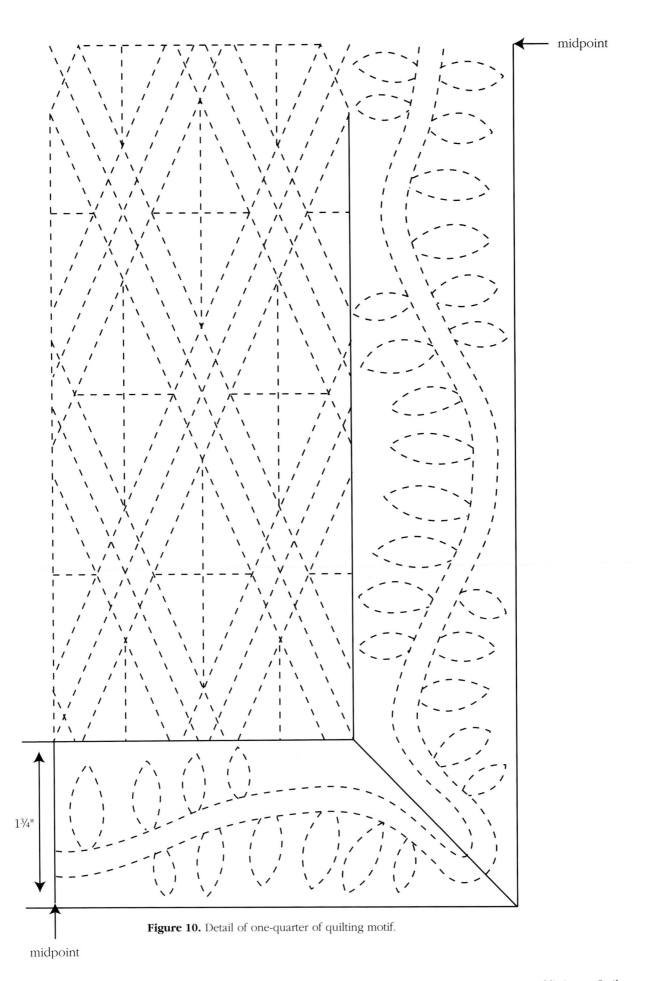

midpoint

1¾"

midpoint

Figure 10. Detail of one-quarter of quilting motif.

Figure 11. Entire quilting layout for *Provençial Wedding Quilt.*

Chapter Two

Medallions or Framed Quilts

Plate 24.

YARDAGE:
1⅜ yd. white (includes backing)
½ yd. red
¼ yd. green

CUT:
Cut the following from the templates on pages 33 – 35.
Template A – 1 green
Template B – 1 green
Template B – 1 red
Template C – 1 green
Template D – 2 red
Template D – 1 green
Template E –1 red
Template F – 1 green
Template G – 28 green
Template G – 25 red
Template H – 4 green
Template I – 4 white
Template J – 24 white
Template J – 16 red
Template K – 4 green
Template L – 8 green
Template L – 4 red
Template M – 8 red

SKILL LEVEL: *Advanced*

DURHAM APPLIQUÉ MEDALLION QUILT
Plate: 6

Dimensions: 28" x 28"
Number of Pieces: 268
Construction Techniques: Pieced and Appliqué
Fabrics: Solid white, solid green, and small red print

DIRECTIONS:

Medallion assembly: Stitch two green borders to opposite sides of center white square in a slightly generous seam allowance (the width of a stitching line). Add red squares to the ends of both remaining green border strips. Attach these units to the center

Cutting instructions continued
Template M – 4 green
Template N – 4 green
Template N – 4 red
Template P – 4 red
Template P – 4 green

32" of ⅝" wide strips of green on bias, cut into lengths to match stems in center square
52" of ½" wide strips of green on bias, cut into lengths to match stems in corner squares, OR green embroidery floss in the same shade as the green fabric

1 – 8" square, white
8 – 1" squares, red
4 – 6½" x 6½" x 9" triangles, red
4 – 1" x 8" strips, green
4 – 1" x 12½" strips, green
8 – 2" x 13½" strips, white
4 – 2" x 13½" strips, red
4 – 2" x 22½" strips, red
4 – 2" x 25½" strips, white
4 – 4½" squares, white
16 – ¾" x 4½" strips, green
16 – ¾" squares, red
4 – 2" squares, white
4 – 2 squares, red
1 – 30" square for backing

square, using the same seam allowance as above. Stitch four red triangles to the center square, using the same seam allowance as on center square. *Do not use generous seam allowance again.* Add green borders and red corner squares to the enlarged central square.

Sew one short white border to one short red border. Add another short white border to the other side of the red border. See assembly diagram Fig. 12. Repeat this step three more times, creating a three stripe unit for each side of the central square.

Attach green borders with red corner squares to each of the 4½" squares. Attach two of the three stripe border units to the opposite sides of the central square. Stitch two of the completed border corner blocks to the opposite ends of the two remaining border stripe units and attach these to the center square.

Stitch two of the long red border strips to the opposite sides of the enlarged center. Attach two 2" squares to opposite ends of the two remaining red strips. Attach these units to the quilt top. Repeat this process with the remaining white border strips and red corner squares.

Appliqué: The appliqué work is begun only after the quilt top is assembled. This technique will reduce stretching on the various small units that compose the quilt. Using the full-size appliqué diagrams provided, mark the placement of appliqué on the center squares (fig. 13), corner triangles (fig. 14), all corner blocks (fig. 15), and borders (fig. 16). Beginning in the center, apply the stems to the white center square. (Use the appliqué method with which you are the most comfortable.) The stems should measure ³⁄₁₆" wide when finished.

Add flower pot, flowers, and leaves, in that order.

Appliqué the buds and stars to the four red triangles. Next apply the stars to the outside borders and corner squares. Appliqué stems to four corner blocks. The stems should measure ⅛" in width. If this is too difficult, embroider stems with four strands of floss using a chain stitch. Appliqué flower pot, flowers, and leaves in that order.

Quilting: Beginning in the center square, quilt around all appliqué shapes and along pieced seams. Quilt in the flower pot and in some of the flowers as indicated in the diagrams. Using the template shape provided, quilt scallops along border edges.

Quilt around appliqué motifs in the four corner triangles and along all pieced seams and inside appliqué shapes when indicated on templates. Quilt the background of the four triangles in parallel rows ½" apart.

Quilt in a cable pattern in each border (fig.17), quilting around stars and along pieced seams to enhance shapes.

Quilt along the pieced seams in the four corner appliqué blocks, and around all appliquéd shapes. Quilt inside the flower pot and flowers as indicated in the diagrams.

Finishing: Use technique "A," see page 8. It will not be possible to quilt a row ¼" from the finished edge as it would run into the cable pattern.

13" finished size

13" finished size

13" finished size

22" finished size

25" finished size

Figure 12. Assembly diagram used to create the striped borders on the *Durham Appliqué Medallion Quilt.*

Figure 13. Center block placement guide for appliqué pieces and quilting lines.

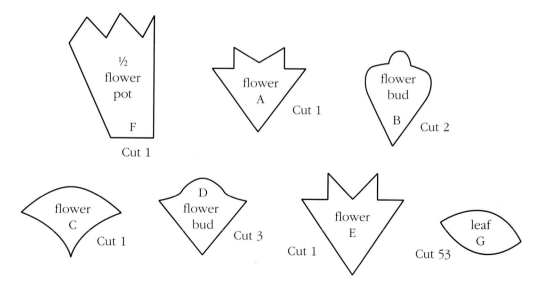

Durham Appliqué Medallion center block templates
Templates do not include seam allowances.

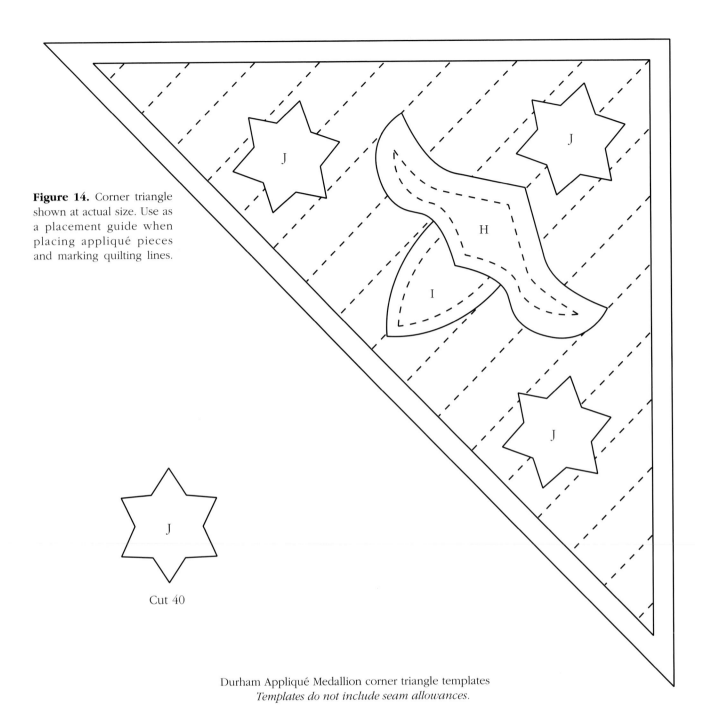

Figure 14. Corner triangle shown at actual size. Use as a placement guide when placing appliqué pieces and marking quilting lines.

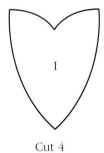

J

Cut 40

Durham Appliqué Medallion corner triangle templates
Templates do not include seam allowances.

I

Cut 4

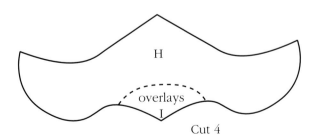

H

overlays
I

Cut 4

Figure 15. Corner block for *Durham Appliqué Medallion Quilt.* Rotate block with flowers pointed outward for all four corners.

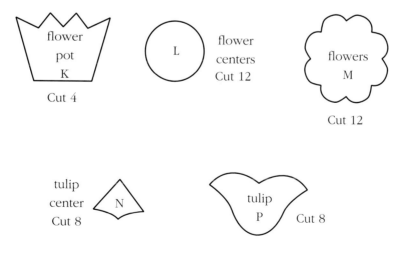

Durham Appliqué Medallion corner block templates
Templates do not include seam allowances.

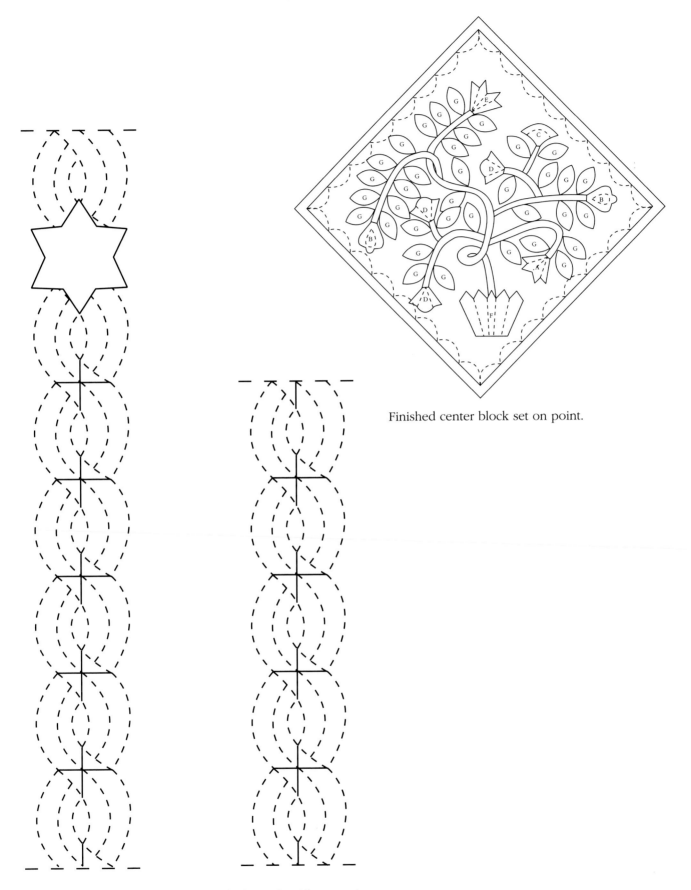

Finished center block set on point.

Figure 16. Diagram and placement guide for appliquéd stars and cable quilting templates used in the borders. Shown actual size.

— center of border

Figure 17. Quilting diagram for *Durham Appliqué Medallion Quilt.*

Plate 25.

YARDAGE:

Scraps to total ¼ yd. light prints
¼ yd. dark prints
⅜ yd. blue prints
⅝ yd. backing and binding

CUT:

1 – 2¼" square of blue print
36 – 1½" squares from blue print
96 – 1½" x 2¼" rectangles from dark prints
82 – 1½" x 2¼" rectangles from light prints
142 – 1½" x ¾" "spacers" from blue prints
1 rectangle 19½" x 23" for backing

SKILL LEVEL: *Intermediate*

WELSH SCRAP MEDALLION QUILT
Plate 7

Dimensions: 17¾" x 21¾"
Number of Pieces: 357
Construction Technique: Pieced
Fabrics: Dark blue prints, light and dark prints

DIRECTIONS:

Row 1: Sew one light rectangle to either side of the large blue square.

Row 2: Sew one small blue square to either end of a light rectangle.

Row 3: Repeat row 2. Assemble these three rows into a Nine-Patch block. See assembly diagram, Fig. 18.

Using Plate 7 and assembly the diagram, assemble alternating light and dark rows, both vertically and horizontally. In rows 2 through 15, each corner should have a small blue square. Rows 16 and 17 do not end with a blue square, but instead end with a light rectangle. Rows 18 and 19 will end with a small blue square.

Be careful when seaming small blue "spacers." Be sure to keep seam lines straight and of equal width.

Quilting: Quilt in-the-ditch around all patches.

Finishing: Technique "B," see page 8.

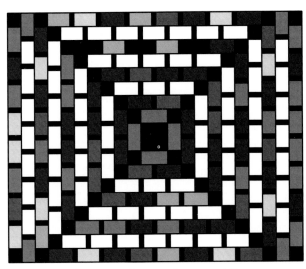

Figure 18. Placement diagram for assembling rows and Nine-Patch center block for *Welsh Scrap Medallion Quilt.*

Plate 26.

YARDAGE:

Scraps
2½" square multicolor stripe
2 strips 1½" x 6½" green stripe
2 – 2½" squares yellow/green print
2 strips 1½" x 6½" small green check
2 strips 1½" x 4½" multicolor print
2 strips 1½" x 9" small green plaid
2 strips 1½" x 3½" larger green plaid
2 strips 2" x 4" light green solid
⅛ yd. rust red solid
⅛ yd. medium green solid
⅛ yd. dark green solid
½ yd. (backing) green plaid

CUT:

1 – 2½" square multicolor stripe
2 – 2½" squares yellow/green print
2 – 1½" x 6½" strips check
2 – 1½" x 4½" strips multicolor print
2 – 1½" x 8½" strips rust red solid
2 – 1½" x 6½" strips rust red solid
2 – 1½" x 9" strips small green plaid
2 – 1½" x 3½" strips larger green plaid
2 – 1½" x 6½" strips green stripe
4 – 2" x 8½" strips medium green solid
4 – 2" x 4" strips light green solid
2 – 2" x 15½" strips rust red solid
2 – 2" x 14½" strips dark green solid
1 – 16" x 20" rectangle for backing

SKILL LEVEL: *Beginner*

SWEDISH FRAMED MEDALLION
Plate 8

Dimensions: 14" x 18"
Number of Pieces: 29
Construction Technique: Pieced
Fabrics: Multicolor stripe, green stripe, yellow/green print, small green check, multicolor print, rust red solid, small green plaid, larger green plaid, light green solid, medium green solid, dark green solid, and green plaid for backing

DIRECTIONS:

Using assembly diagram Fig. 19 as your guide, construct as follows:

Row 1. Sew the two yellow/green print squares to either side of the multicolor center square.

Row 2 & 3. Sew check strips to either side of row 1.

Row 4 & 5. Sew multicolor print to top and bottom of center unit.

Row 6 & 7. Sew long rust strips to sides of center unit.

Row 8 & 9. Sew short rust strips to top and bottom of center unit.

Row 10 & 11. Sew green stripe strips to top and bottom of center unit.

Row 12 & 13. Sew one small green plaid strip to one large green plaid strip. Repeat for remaining strips. Attach each of these strips to sides of center unit.

Row 14 & 15. Sew two of the 8½" lengths of medium green to top and bottom of center unit.

Row 16 & 17. Sew one of each of the light green strips to either side of the two remaining medium green strips. Attach these to the center unit.

Row 18 & 19. Sew the remaining rust strips to either side of the center unit.

Row 20 & 21. Sew dark green strips to top and bottom of quilt.

Quilting: Quilt in the ditch along all seam lines. In the wider outside rows, quilt a line of stitching through the center of each row using matching color quilting thread.

Finishing: Use technique "A," see page 8. Do not quilt ¼" from edge.

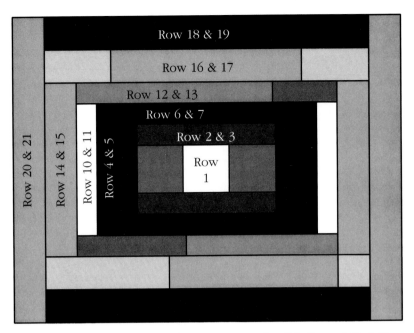

Figure 19. Assembly diagram for constructing *Swedish Framed Medallion Quilt.* Refer to sewing directions on the previous page for color selections.

Chapter Three

Strippy Quilts

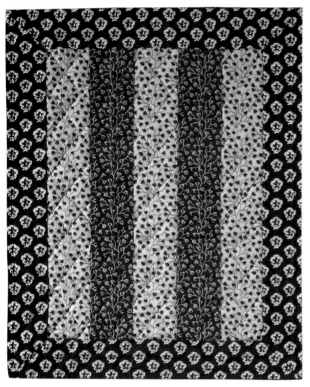

Plate 27.

SKILL LEVEL: *Beginner*

PROVENÇAL STRIPPY QUILT
Plate 9

Dimensions: 13" x 16"
Number of Pieces: 9
Construction Techniques: Pieced
Fabrics: Small red print, small yellow print (same motif or different), and a larger red print for border

DIRECTIONS:

Sew alternating red and yellow strips to create center. Add borders extending the extra length evenly beyond all seams. Miter corners and trim square. See Plate 9.

Quilting: The quilting is an over-all crosshatching pattern (Fig. 20). Begin in the upper right corner and quilt in a straight line to the lower left corner. Do not quilt out to the edge, stop ½" from all edges. Quilt in parallel rows 1" apart on either side of the first row until the entire surface is completed. Repeat the procedure in the opposite direction.

Finishing: Technique "A," see page 8. After finishing, quilt ¼" from edge on all sides.

YARDAGE:

½ yd. red strips and backing
¼ yd. yellow strips (½ yd. if fabric is directional)
¼ yd. red borders (½ yd. if fabric is directional)

CUT:

1 – 15" x 18" rectangle for backing on the cross grain (unless directional fabric)
2 – 2½" x 13½" strips red
3 – 2½" x 13½" strips yellow borders: on the cross grain (unless directional fabric)
2 – 2" x 14½"
2 – 2" x 17½"

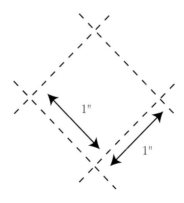

Figure 20. Allover crosshatching quilting diagram for *Provençal Strippy Quilt.*

Plate 28.

SWEDISH STRIPPY QUILT
Plate 10

Dimensions: 15¾" x 19¼"
Number of Pieces: 87 (approximate)
Construction Technique: Pieced
Fabrics: Stripes, ticking-like fabrics, plaids, checks, small prints

DIRECTIONS:

Sew various lengths of each width together to create rows 14½" long. These will be sewn to each other alternating width of rows. See Plate 10. Try to avoid having seams of different pieces line up evenly. Spontaneity is an important component of this quilt.

When the rows total 9½" wide, attach two rows made from the 2½" wide strips to the sides. Attach another wide row to the bottom and a narrow row to the top made from the 2" wide strips.

Quilting: Quilt along seam lines and through the middle of some rows, both horizontally and vertically. After completing the edge finishing, quilt along the edge of the backing where it meets the front. Quilt along binding miter seams.

Finishing: Bring the back over the front and trim to create a second "border" of different widths, trimming batting and backing as necessary. Miter corners. Or trim batting and backing to dimensions of quilt top and use technique "B." See page 8.

YARDAGE:

scraps (about 48 different fabrics)
⅝ yd. for backing

CUT:

strips 1" x various lengths
strips 1½" x various lengths
strips 2" x various lengths for top "border"
strips 2½" x various lengths for side and bottom "borders"
1 rectangle 19" x 22½" for backing

Chapter Four

Hexagons

Plate 29.

YARDAGE:

scraps of many different fabrics
½ yd. for borders and bindings
¾ yd. of light color print for paths
1 yd. for backing

CUT:

646 papers "A"

351 fabric pieces for diamonds: 39 diamonds composed of a center, two from the same fabric for the tips of the diamonds, and six from the same fabric for the rosette, see Fig. 21.

286 fabric pieces for the paths

Borders:
2 – 3¼" x 24¾" strips
2 – 3¼" x 26¼" strips

Backing:
1 – 26" x 28" rectangle

SKILL LEVEL: *Intermediate*

HEXAGON DIAMONDS
Plate 11

Dimensions: 24¾" x 26¼"
Number of Pieces: 646
Construction Technique: Paper Pieced and Appliquéd
Fabrics: Brown, rusts, reds, and beige prints in small nondescript and distinct prints

DIRECTIONS:

Cut out fabric and papers. Wrap fabric over papers as described in the General Information Section. Stitch the hexagons together to form diamonds, see Plate 11. After all the diamonds have been constructed, lay them out in four rows of six diamond units with alternating rows of five diamond units. Be careful to arrange the diamonds in a pleasing, balanced fashion.

Stitch hexagon paths between and around diamond units using assembly diagram. When the top is completed, remove basting and papers from all but the outside row of hexagons.

Stitch four border pieces together, mitering corners. Baste the top to the borders being careful not to stretch the edges. Appliqué the top to the borders using matching color thread or a middle-value gray thread, removing the remaining basting and papers as you go.

Tying: Lay out backing and cover with a thin batting. Place quilt top over these two layers. Tie a square knot in the middle of each diamond and throughout borders, spacing the ties about three inches apart. Use matching color embroidery floss, three strands thick for the ties.

Finishing: Technique "B," see page 8.

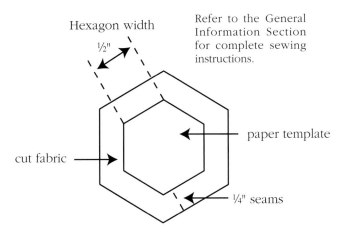

Hexagon width

½"

Refer to the General Information Section for complete sewing instructions.

cut fabric

paper template

¼" seams

Hexagon Diamonds template

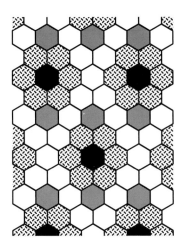

Figure 21. Close-up detail shows how the diamond shape is formed by adding to the top and bottom of the rosette centers.

Figure 22. Placement diagram for the *Hexagon Diamonds Quilt.* Assemble the hexagon paths between the diamond units.

Plate 30.

YARDAGE:
¼ yd. green(s)
scraps orange(s)
scraps beige(s)
¼ yd. pink(s)
scraps yellow(s)
¼ yd. white(s)
¼ yd. brown(s)
¼ yd. rust(s)
⅝ yd. backing

Optional: 2⅛ yd. of ⅛" (or as small as possible) cording for piping ¼ yd. for piping fabric (use one of the fabrics from above)

Cut:
Papers:
473 Template A
20 Template B
44 Template C
4 Template D

Fabric: Cut the following from the templates on page 46.
95 Template A green
8 Template B green

TRIP AROUND THE WORLD HEXAGONS QUILT
Plate 12

Dimensions: 16¾" x 20¾"
Number of Pieces: 541
Construction Technique: Paper Pieced
Fabrics: This quilt can be made with one print fabric in each of the listed colors, but a much richer quilt results when more than one print fabric in each color family is used.

DIRECTIONS:
Cut out fabric and papers. Wrap the fabric over the papers as described in the General Information Section. Begin assembly at the center of the quilt using the diagram provided, Fig. 23. When the top is completely assembled, remove basting and papers from all hexagons except those along the outside edge.

Piping: See *Finishing* in General Information.

Removing the papers all at once would distort the shape of this quilt. Do not attempt to machine sew the piping on this quilt. Baste the piping to the quilt top, removing papers as you come to them. Using an appliqué stitch, hand sew the piping to the quilt top.

Tying: Cut the batting to fit and lay out the quilt top on the batting placed on top of the backing. Baste the three layers together. Using three strands of embroidery floss, tie the quilt either on front or back.

Finishing: Trim backing and fold in ¼" seam allowance. Stitch the backing to the piping as on the top of the quilt.

8 Template C green
6 Template A orange
18 template A beige
84 Template A pink
4 Template B pink
4 Template C pink
30 Template A yellow
96 Template A white
82 Template A brown
4 Template B brown
4 Template C brown
62 Template A rust
4 Template B rust
28 Template C rust
4 Template D rust
1 – 19" x 23" rectangle for backing

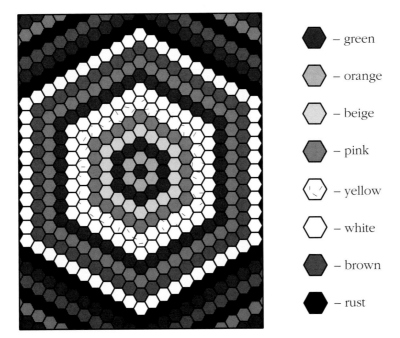

- green
- orange
- beige
- pink
- yellow
- white
- brown
- rust

Figure 23. Assembly diagram for *Trip Around the World Hexagon Quilt.* Start joining colored hexagons in the center and work outward toward the straight edges.

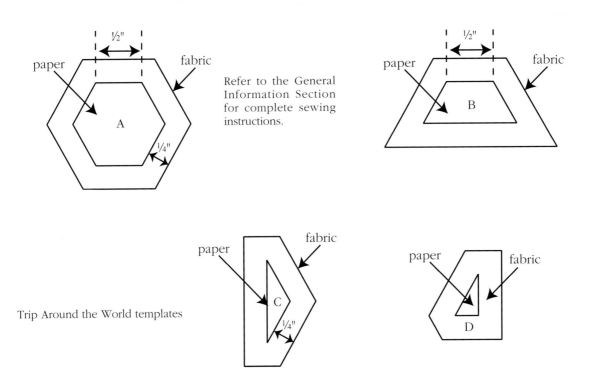

Refer to the General Information Section for complete sewing instructions.

paper   fabric

A   ½"   ¼"

paper   fabric

B   ½"

Trip Around the World templates

paper   fabric

C   ¼"

paper   fabric

D

Chapter Five

Log Cabin

Plate 31.

YARDAGE:

¾ yd. red
¼ yd. white
Optional: 1½ yds. edging

CUT:

16 – ¾" squares red
16 – ¾" squares white
32 – ½" x 1" red
32 – ½" x 1¼" white
32 – ½" x 1½" red
32 – ½" x 1¾" white
32 – ½" x 2" red
32 – ½" x 2¼" white
32 – ½" x 2½" red
16 – ½" x 2¾" white

Borders:
4 – 1¾" x 11" red

Backing:
1 – 13" square red

SKILL LEVEL: *Intermediate*

SCOTTISH RED AND WHITE LOG CABIN QUILT
Plate 13

Dimensions: 12½" x 12½"
Number of Pieces: 276
Construction Technique: Pieced
Fabrics: Red and white cotton
Optional: lace, crochet work, or other type of edging, 1" to 1½" wide.

DIRECTIONS:

Using the block assembly, Fig. 24, pieces can be sewn in the traditional method starting with the middle square. Or, trace the assembly diagram and use the modern paper foundation method.

Stitch four blocks together to form a row. There are four rows. Use the assembly diagram Fig. 25 for block arrangement. Add borders, mitering corners.

Optional: Lace, crochet work, or other edging can be added to borders for embellishment.

Tying: Tie on the reverse side of the quilt using one strand of embroidery floss. Be careful to hide the base of the tie at a seam joint so that it will not interfere with the design on the front of the quilt.

Finishing: Use technique "A," see page 8.

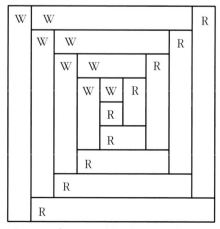

Figure 24. Assembly diagram for Log Cabin block using red and white fabrics.

Figure 25. Overall assembly diagram for the *Scottish Red and White Log Cabin Quilt.* Follow this placement guide when joining each row of blocks.

Plate 32.

YARDAGE:

scraps

½ yd. red print for borders and backing

¼ yd. solid red for center square

CUT:

5½" square for center – solid red

4 – 1½" squares for center – red plaid

assorted strips of varying widths and lengths

Borders:

2 – 1¾" x 9½" sides – red print

2 – 5" x 12" top and bottom – red print

SWEDISH LOG CABIN VARIATION QUILT
Plate 14

Dimensions: 11½" x 18"

Number of Pieces: 77 (approximate)

Construction Technique: Pieced

Fabrics: Assorted plaids, checks, and prints in various colors. (My quilt contains 29 different fabrics.)

DIRECTIONS:

Starting with one of the 1½" squares, attach strips of various widths to each of the four sides until a 2½" square is achieved. Repeat this procedure with the three remaining squares. Use some of the same fabrics and introduce others. These blocks become the Log Cabin corners.

Assemble the remaining scraps into rows 5½" long. Stitch rows together to equal 2½" wide. Attach two of these units to the top and bottom of the center square. Stitch a Log Cabin block to either end of each remaining side unit. Attach these to the center square. Add the top and bottom borders. Remember, the bottom border is wider than the top. See Plate 14.

Quilting: Following the quilting diagram, Fig. 26, quilt a chevron pattern in the center square in rows ½" apart. Quilt in the ditch along the outside seams of the center square, through the middle of the pieced borders, and in the ditch along the edge of the outside borders. Quilt in parallel rows about 1" apart in the top and bottom borders, ending in a line that would be the extension of the outside borders.

Finishing: Technique "A," see page 8.

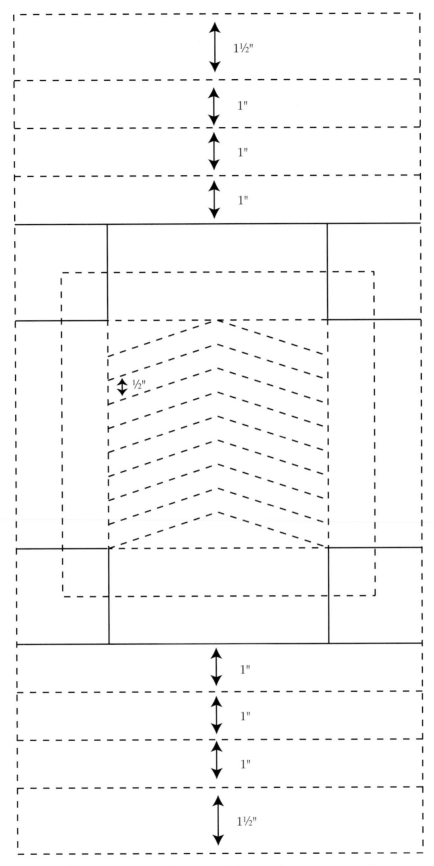

Figure 26. Quilting diagram for the *Swedish Log Cabin Variation Quilt.*

Chapter Six

Provençal One Patch

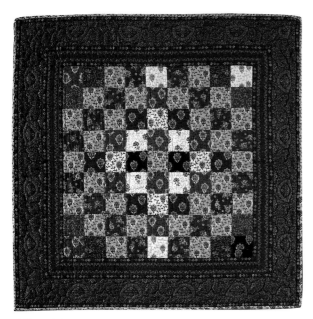

Plate 33.

YARDAGE:

scraps

½ yd. for backing

CUT:

81 – 2" squares

4 – 3" x 22" strips for borders (approximate, depends upon width of strips used for border)

1 – 22" square backing

SKILL LEVEL: *Beginner*

PROVENÇAL ONE PATCH QUILT
Plate 15

Dimensions: 20¾" x 20¾" (exact size depends upon the width of the border print)

Number of Pieces: 85

Construction Technique: Pieced

Fabrics: Small floral prints and stripe for border

DIRECTIONS:

Lay out the squares in a pleasing pattern. It is easiest to pick the print you like best for the center and then arrange the others around it. My arrangement is similar to the traditional American quilt pattern One Patch Trip Around the World (see Plate 15). When you are happy with your arrangement, sew nine squares together to form a row. Assemble nine rows and add borders. Miter corners.

Quilting: Quilt in the ditch around each of the squares. Quilt the border following the pattern of the print, accentuating its design features.

Finishing: Technique "B," see page 8.

Chapter Seven

Tumbling Blocks

Plate 34.

TUMBLING BLOCKS OR BABY'S BLOCKS
Plate 16

Dimensions: 8½" x 14¼" without edging
Number of Pieces: 295
Construction Technique: Paper Pieced
Fabrics: Silks, solids, and prints

DIRECTIONS:

Wrap silk over papers. Using a medium gray color thread (silk is preferable, but regular sewing thread will do), whipstitch the diamond shapes together on the reverse.

Assemble one diamond each of light, medium, and dark patches to form a cube shape. See the assembly diagram, Fig. 27. Make 85 of these. Keeping the light, medium, and dark facing in the same direction, assemble these cubes into seven rows of seven cubes and six rows of six cubes. Sew the quilt top together by alternating rows. Complete the top by attaching half diamonds – "B" to side edges, "C" to top and bottom edges, and "D" to the four corners. See the assembly diagram, Fig. 28.

When the top is complete, clip basting and remove all papers except those along the outside edges.

Tying: Use the thinnest batting you can buy. If necessary, split a thicker bat. Matching the color of the backing, use a single strand of embroidery floss

YARDAGE:

scraps of light, medium, and dark silks
  (I used 70 different fabrics.)
⅜ yd. backing (silk is preferable, but a fine cotton
  can also be used)

CUT:

Papers:
255 Template A
24 Template B
12 Template C
4 Template D

Fabric:
85 Template A from light
85 Template A from medium
85 Template A from dark
24 Template B for sides
12 Template C for top and bottom
4 Template D for corners
1 – 9½" x 15¼" rectangle for backing

Miniature Quilts

to tie the quilt on the reverse side. To avoid tacking stitches from showing on the front, make ties at the joints of the cubes.

Finishing: If edging is desired, sew trim to the edge of the quilt. Be sure to keep the seam to the inside. Trim backing ¼" larger than the front of the quilt. Tuck in and hand sew closed. Remove tacking and papers in each piece as you stitch backing to it. If you remove the papers too soon, the outside edges may distort.

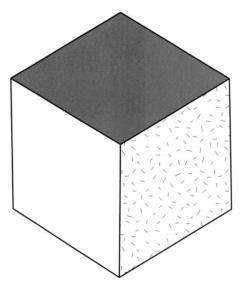

Figure 27. A diamond cube made of light, medium, and dark patches.

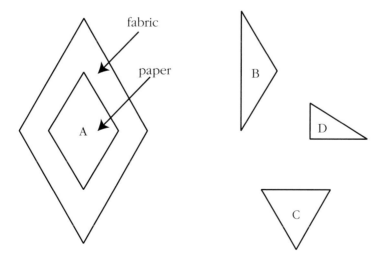

Tumbling Blocks templates
Templates do not include seam allowance.

Figure 28. Assembly diagram for *Tumbling Blocks* (*Baby's Blocks*).

Chapter Eight

Elizabeth Sanderson Star

Plate 35.

YARDAGE:

⅝ yd. white (1⅜ yd. if backing is included)
½ yd. pink
¾ yd. backing (if not using white)

CUT:

Papers:
8 Template A without seam allowance
8 Template B without seam allowance

Fabric:
8 Template A from white
8 Template B from pink
1 – 12" square from white
2 strips 1½" x 12" from pink
2 strips 1½" x 14" from pink
2 strips 2¼" x 14" from white
2 strips 2¼" x 17½" from white
2 strips 1½" x 17½" from pink
2 strips 1½" x 19½" from pink
2 strips 2¼" x 19½" from white
2 strips 2¼" x 23" from white
2 strips 2¼" x 23" from pink
2 strips 2¼" x 26½" from pink

SKILL LEVEL: *Advanced*

ELIZABETH SANDERSON STAR QUILT
Plate 17

Dimensions: 26" x 26"
Number of Pieces: 37
Construction Technique(s): Hand and Machine Piecing and Appliqué
Fabrics: Pink, medium blue, or turkey red and white

DIRECTIONS:

Using the paper-piecing technique in the General Directions, piece inner-most star. Complete by adding outer star pieces. See the assembly diagram, Fig. 29.

Using the assembly diagram Fig. 30, construct as follows:

Row 1 pink: Add the 1½" x 12" strips to the opposite sides of the 12" center square. Add the 1½" x 14" strips to the two remaining sides.

Row 2 white: Add the 2¼" x 14" top and bottom strips. Continue by adding the 2¼" x 17½" strips to sides.

Row 3 pink: Add the 1½" x 17½" top and bottom strips. Continue by adding the 1½" x 19½" strips to sides.

Row 4 white: Add the 2¼" x 19½" top and bottom strips. Continue by adding the 2¼" x 23" strips to sides.

Row 5 pink: Add the 2¼" x 23" top and bottom strips. Continue by adding the 2¼" x 26½" strips to sides.

After the top is constructed, appliqué the star to the center square.

Quilting: Quilt the top using the quilting layout, Fig. 31. Quilt along seam lines. You may simplify your quilt by altering or substituting your quilting patterns for some or all of those provided.

Finishing: Technique "B," see page 8.

Figure 29. Assembly diagram for the *Elizabeth Sanderson Star Quilt* pieces.

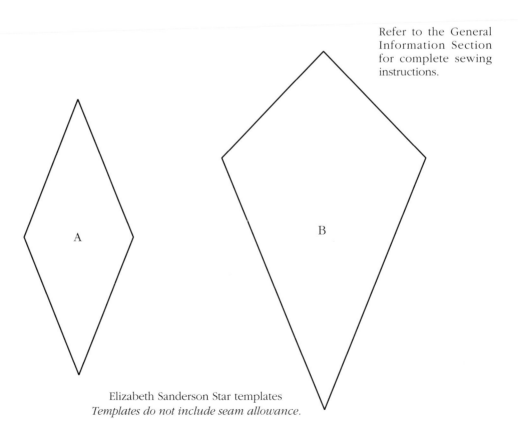

Refer to the General Information Section for complete sewing instructions.

A

B

Elizabeth Sanderson Star templates
Templates do not include seam allowance.

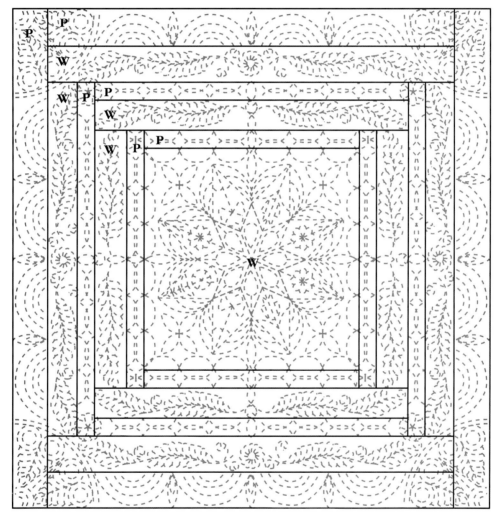

Figure 30. Assembly diagram for the *Elizabeth Sanderson Star Quilt* using white and pink fabrics. Illustrated with complete quilting design layout.

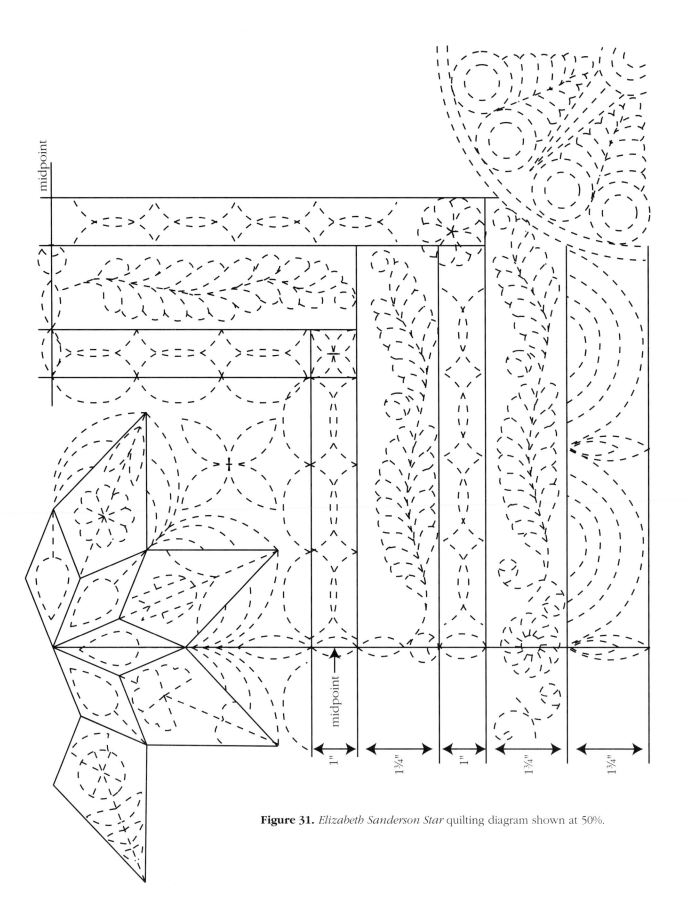

Figure 31. *Elizabeth Sanderson Star* quilting diagram shown at 50%.

Chapter Nine

Octagons

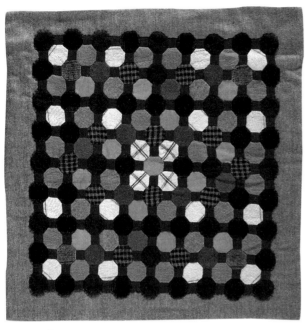

Plate 36.

YARDAGE:

¼ yd. dark fabric or scraps
¼ yd. light fabric or scraps
¼ yd. red
½ yd. for borders and backing

CUT:

Papers:
145 Template A without seam allowance
144 Template B without seam allowance

Fabric:
80 Template A dark
65 Template A light
144 Template B
15" x 15" square for backing
15" x 15" square for border

SKILL LEVEL: *Advanced*

Octagons
Plate 18

Dimensions: 14½" x 14½"
Number of Pieces: 289
Construction Techniques: Hand Pieced and Appliqué
Fabrics: Cottons, checks and plaids, and solids, optional: wools and flannels. Be careful, as these fabrics distort very easily.

DIRECTIONS:

Wrap fabric over papers and baste (as in General Directions). Start in the center and piece according to the assembly diagram Fig. 32.

When the octagons are assembled, remove basting and papers from all but the outside rows. Lay patchwork on top of the border square and appliqué in place, removing papers as each octagon is sewn down. Cut away fabric from behind the patchwork leaving a ¼" seam allowance.

Tying and Quilting: On the back, tie the three layers together using three strands of embroidery floss. Quilt around the outside row of octagons and squares.

Finishing: Technique "A," see page 8.

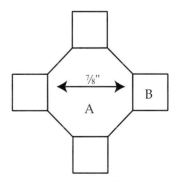

Octagon templates
Templates do not include seam allowances.

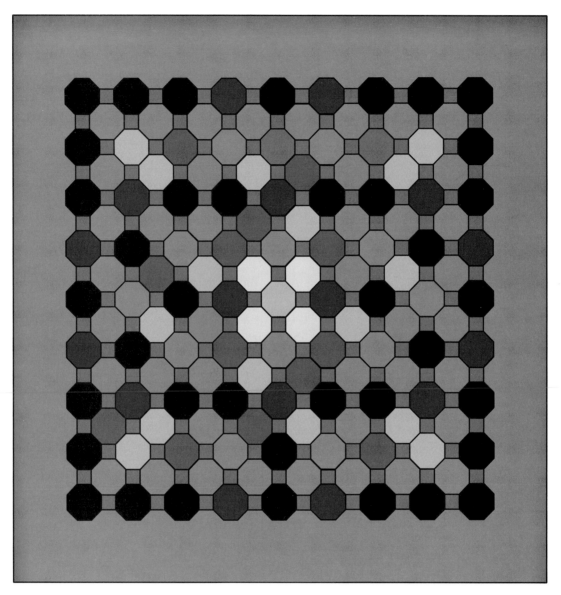

Figure 32. Assembly diagram for the *Octagon Quilt.* Start in the center and piece outwards. The last rows are appliquéd to the borders.

Bibliography

Allan, Rosemary E. *Quilts and Coverlets from Beamish Museum County Durham.* Beamish North of England Open Air Museum, 1987.

Arnolli, Gieneke & Systske Wille-Engelsma. *Sits, Exotishch Textiel in Friesland* (Chintz, Exotic Textiles in Friesland). Waanders Uitgevers, Zwolle, 1990.

Aspin, Chris. *The Cotton Industry,* Shire Album #63. Buckinghamshire: Shire Publications Ltd., 1981.

Biehn, Michel. *En Jupon Piqué et Robe D'Indienne, Costumes Provencaux.* Maquette Arbook International, 1987.

Brédif, Josette. *Printed French Fabrics, Toiles de Jouy.* NY: Rizzoli International Publications, Inc., l989.

Clabburn, Pamela. *Patchwork,*Shire Album #101. Buckinghamshire: Shire Publications Ltd., 1983.

_____. *Shawls.* Shire Album #77. Buckinghamshire: Shire Publicatons Ltd., 1981.

Clark, Hazel. *Textile Printing,* Shire Album #135. Buckinghamshire: Shire Publications Ltd.,1985.

Colby, Averil. *Patchwork.* Newton MA: Charles T. Branford Co., 1958.

_____. *Patchwork Quilts.* NY: Charles Scribner's Sons, 1965.

_____. *Quilting.* NY: Charles Scribner's Sons, 1971.

Collins, Louanne. *Silk Museums in Macclesfield.* Village, Huntington, York, 1989.

FitzRandolph, Mavis & Florence M. Fletcher. *Quilting, Traditional Methods and Design.* Leicester: Dryad Press, 1955.

Ginsburg, Madeleine (Ed.). *The Illustrated History of Textiles.* London: Studio Editions Ltd., 1991.

von Gwinner, Schnuppe. *The History of the Patchwork Quilt, Origins, Traditions and Symbols of a Textile Art.* West Chester, PA: Schiffer Publishing Ltd., 1988.

Hake, Elizabeth. *English Quilting, Old & New.* B.T. Batsford Ltd., 1937.

Jerde, Judith. *Encyclopedia of Textiles.* NY: Facts on File Inc., 1992.

Langley, Lloyd. *Our Chapel.* Beamish, The North of England Open Air Museum.

Marchbank, Brenda. *Durham Quilting.* London: Dryad Press Ltd., 1988.

Meulenbelt-Nieuwburg, A. *Onder de Dekens, Tussen de Lakens...(Under the Blankets, Between the Sheets...).* The Netherlands Openlucht Museum, Arnhem, 1981.

Moonem, An. *Quilts een Nederlandse Traditie* (Quilts, The Dutch Tradition). The Netherlands Openlucht Museum, Arnhem, 1992.

Osler, Dorothy. *Traditional British Quilts.* London: B.T. Bratsford, Ltd., 1978.

Paisley Shawls. Renfrew Museum and Art Galleries Services, Renfrew District Council, Paisley Scotland.

Parker, Freda. *Victorian Patchwork.* North Pomfret, VT: Tralfalgar Square Publishing, 1992.

Parry, Linda, (Ed.). *A Practical Guide to Patchwork from the Victoria and Albert Museum.* Pittstown, NJ: The Main Street Press, 1987.

Patchwork & Quilting in Scotland 1760-1984, An exhibition organized by Thistle Quilters and the Edinburgh City Museums and Art Galleries Catalogue. Thistle Quilters, 1984.

Quilting. Information Sheet; Beamish, The North of England Open Air Museum, 1987.

Rae, Janet. *The Quilts of the British Isles.* NY: E. P. Dutton, 1987.

Reilly, Valerie. *The Paisley Pattern, The Official Illustrated History.* Salt Lake City: Gibbs Smith, 1987.

Schoeser, Mary & Kathleen Dejardin. *French Textiles from 1760 to the Present.* Laurence King Ltd., 1991.

Schoeser, Mary & Celia Rufey. *English and American Textiles from 1790 to the Present.* NY: Thames and Hudson Inc., 1989.

Seward, Linda. *Country Quilts.* London: Mitchell Beazley International, Ltd., 1992.

Shearer, David R. *Why Paisley?* Scotland: Paisley Museum and Art Galleries, Paisley, 1985.

Stevens, Christine. *Quilts.* Gomer Press in association with the National Museum of Wales, 1993.

Walker, Michele. *Good Housekeeping Patchwork and Appliqué.* London: Ebury Press, 1981.

_____. *Quilting & Patchwork.* NY: Ballantine Books, 1983.

_____. *The Passionate Quilter.* London: Ebury Press, 1990.

Wettre, Åsa. *Gamla Svenska Lapptäcken.* Stockholm: Tidens förlag, 1993.

William, Eurwyn. *Rhyd-Y-Car, A Welsh Mining Community.* National Museum of Wales in conjunction with D. Brown and Sons Ltd., Cowbridge, 1987.

Museums which exhibit quilts
& other historic textiles

ENGLAND
Abbott Hall Museum of Lakeland
  Life and Industry
Abbott Hall
Kendal, Cumbria

American Museum in Britain
Claverton Manor
Bath, Avon BA2 7BD

Jane Austen's Home
Chawton
Alton, Hampshire

Blists Hill Open Air Museum
Ironbridge
Telford, Shropshire TF8 7RE

Bowes Museum
Barnard Castle
County Durham

The Cambridge and County
  Folk Museum
2 Castle Street
Cambridge CB3 0AQ

Gawthorpe Hall
Padiham, Nr Burnley
Lancashire BB12 8UA

Castle Howard Costumes Galleries
The Stables
Castle Howard, York

Levens Hall
Kendall, Cumbria LA8 0PB

Museum of Costume
Assembly Rooms
Bath, Avon BA1 2EW

North of England Open
  Air Museum
Beamish, Stanley
County Durham DH9 0RG

Quarrybank Mill
Styal, Wilmslow
Cheshire SK9 4LA
(Museum of the Cotton Industry)

Strangers Hall
Charing Cross
Norwich, Norfolk NR2 4AL

Victoria and Albert Museum
Cromwell Road
South Kensington
London SW7 2RI

Witworth Art Gallery
University of Manchester
Oxford Rd
Manchester

Worthington Museum and
  Art Gallery
Chapel Road
Worthington, West Sussex

WALES
Brecknock Museum
Brecon, Powys

Welsh Folk Museum
St. Fagans
Cardiff CF4 6XB

SCOTLAND
Fife Folk Museum
Ceres, Nr. Cupar
Fife

Paisley Museum and Art Galleries
High Street
Paisley PA1 2BA

Traquair
Innerleithen
Peebles

NORTHERN IRELAND
Ulster Folk and Transport Museum
Cultra Manor
Holywood
Co. Down BT18 0EU

FRANCE
Museé Charles Demery
Souleiado
39, rue Proudhon
13150 Tarascon

Museé Municipal de la Toile
  de Jouy
54, rue Charles de Gaulle
Jouy en Josas

NETHERLANDS
Nederlands Openluchtmuseum
Schelmseweg 89
6816 SJ Arnhem

SWEDEN
Nordiska Museet
Djurgardsvägen 6-16
Djurgarden, S-11521

Röhsska Konstslöjd Museet
(The Museum of Applied Art)
Box 53178
Vasag 37-39
S-40015 Göteborg

Skansen
Djurgarden S-11521
Stockholm
(Open Air Museum)

Textil Museet
Boras

Textilmuseet
Högbo

*Please write ahead, some museums do
not keep textiles on permanent display
and an appointment must be made to
view these items.

MORE Great Books by the
Miniature Quilt Expert Tina Gravatt

Heirloom Miniatures

64 pages, 8½" x 11". #2097
(ISBN: 0-89145-957-X) $9.95

OLD FAVORITES In Miniature

Patterns & Instructions for Making
Nineteen Miniature Quilts

by Tina Gravatt

104 pages, 8½" x 11". #3469 (ISBN: 0-89145-808-5) $15.95

BUY BOTH AND SAVE!

Join famous author and columnist for *Lady's Circle Patchwork Quilts* magazine as she shares her collection of miniature patterns from around the world. Quilters will enjoy re-creating the history of quilting in miniature.

Collectors everywhere are fascinated by the charm of doll and miniature quilts! Explore the different styles and vintage fabrics used in constructing historically accurate miniature quilts in this ongoing series by the well-known quilting authority, Tina Gravatt. Her first book, **Heirloom Miniatures**, features 17 colorful quilts from Grandmother's Fan to Geese in Flight. Tina's second book, **Old Favorites in Miniatures**, has 19 more scaled-to-perfection patterns, such as Delectable Mountain, Bethlehem Star, Baltimore Album, and many others. Easy and specific instructions are included in the entire series.

Available at your local bookstores and quilt shops...or order direct from AQS!

#2097 Heirloom Miniatures	$9.95
#3469 Old Favorites in Miniature	$15.95
#4788 2-Volume Set ($4 savings)	$21.90
#4752 Miniature Quilts: Connecting New & Old Worlds	$14.95

To order by mail:
Please enclose $2.00 P & H for the first book and 40¢ for each additional book. KY residents add 6% sales tax.
International postage add $2.50 for first book and $1.00 for each additional book.
Make checks payable to American Quilter's Society.

To order by phone: Monday thru Friday • 8:00-4:00

Order Toll-Free
1-800-626-5420
When Using
Visa & MasterCard

All times central

Miniature Quilts:
Connecting New & Old Worlds by Tina M. Gravatt

Add some miniature European treasures to your collection of little quilts with the help of Tina Gravatt's third book from AQS. The history of the traditional miniatures will unfold as Tina shares 18 patterns from medallions to Log Cabins representing France, the Netherlands, Wales, and other European countries. Colorful illustrations, full-size templates, and quilting diagrams are provided.

64 pages, 8½" x 11". #4752 (ISBN: 0-89145-877-8) $14.95

American Quilter's Society

P. O. Box 3290 • Paducah, KY 42002-3290